CULTURE SHOCK!

A Globe-Trotter's Guide

Frederick Fisher

Graphic Arts Center Publishing Company
Portland, Oregon

In the same series

A Wife's Guide	*Indonesia*	*Singapore*
Australia	*Israel*	*South Africa*
Borneo	*Italy*	*Spain*
Britain	*Japan*	*Sri Lanka*
Burma	*Korea*	*Taiwan*
Canada	*Malaysia*	*Thailand*
China	*Nepal*	*USA*
France	*Norway*	
Hong Kong	*Pakistan*	
India	*Philippines*	

Illustrations by TRIGG
© 1995 Times Editions Pte Ltd

This book is published by special
arrangement with Times Editions Pte Ltd
International Standard Book Number 1-55868-238-4
Library of Congress Catalog 94-799-78
Graphic Arts Center Publishing Company
P.O. Box 10306 • Portland, Oregon 97210 • (503) 226-2402

Printed in Singapore

*To 'Honey', Eileen, for a life together
of near fifty years that grows sweeter
with each new day of travel adventure*

CONTENTS

INTRODUCTION

The *Culture Shock!* version of travel information bridges the gap between mere vacations, and adventures in far away places with strange sounding names. Fears, tremors and trepidations are relieved with common-sense knowledge of how to calm those apprehensions. *The Traveller's Guide* answers hundreds of questions about incidental but important facts. The answers cover how to travel extensively with peace of mind, to enjoy the most remarkable places, to have fun, and to relish the thrill of a high mountain or mighty sea.

How to be an Independent Traveller... tour packages... communications far from home... beat the shocking cost systems and save money... travel agent – friend or foe? These are some of the subjects discussed.

Novice travellers, and people who have undergone a dramatic change or tragedy in their lives, are encouraged to reinvigorate their lifestyles in ways they have probably not thought of. Would-be adventurers who have always bought – or had sold to them – package tours, because it was easier and cheaper that way: they can learn how much more fascinating it is to travel independently, unrestricted by a precise itinerary.

Culture Shock! A Traveller's Guide is for average adults, desiring to have fun and yet be comfortable, in interesting 'dream-about' countries, within their time and budget limits.

Travel adventure is a rare spice for your life.

Chapter One

AND THE DREAMS COME TRUE

The essence is adventure, new horizons, cleansing of the mind, resurgence of health and interest, taste of different foods and regaining the vigour and curiosity of youth. Couples have seen their children grow up and leave home – creating a need to change lifestyle, live it up, see the world. Singles of 40 or over 70, retired, bored, or perhaps lonely from the loss of a mate, are looking for adventure before age cripples the interest – and the body. Rocking-chair blues are setting in as you see friends and neighbours vegetating. Younger folk, like Richard Bach's Jonathan Livingston Seagull, want to try their wings in the stratosphere of the outer world; or are entranced by *Lost Horizon*'s picture of a Shangri-la somewhere out there.

THE ITCH

Never mind why travel and adventure are on your mind; what you feel is like an itch – or like the breeze tickling your nose with an irresistible aroma. Now thoughts of *Where?* and *How?* begin. In the early 20th century, a trip to another continent was made by booking a passage on an ocean liner, crossing countries by train and touring by car in local areas. It was common to allow months or a year for such adventures. Now travellers can be on the other side of the world in under 24 hours from the time they rise in the morning. And at once they enter the ambience of 'Gay Paree', begin to climb the Himalayas in Nepal, take a boat down the Yangtze in China, or land in Singapore and – like that city's Lion – consider where the next thrill will come from.

For novices, whose only experience is a package tour to an island resort, the possibilities parade in the mind's eye. There are the eight wonders of the world to see. Notable destinations are continually being described in travel articles and documentary films. An esoteric whim may move you to the top of the world to climb the hundreds of steps of the Potala Palace in Lhasa, Tibet. Thoughts of plain fun-and-games tempt you to travel to a quiet relaxing beach resort and enjoy the sun and the water, good food and service. Perhaps you like it and want to stay a month. All right. With a deft change in plans, you may learn to snorkel, scuba dive or play tennis. Or more ambitious thoughts may lead you to trek over mild trails or seriously venture through jungles and up mountains. But perhaps what you most want is to soak yourself in a culture on the other side of the world.

SCRATCHING THE ITCH

Inexperienced and shy travellers need a jump-start to help them decide. Maybe the weather or chance dictates, or the mood hits at a decade-marking birthday. There comes a time when one's way of life changes; perhaps on retirement, or on being left at home without children – or a spouse. Single people become aware they are bored with their surroundings and need a new look at life from a different perspective. They hate to admit having been so absorbed in making a living – surviving if you like – that serious travelling is an unknown experience. There is a need for adventurous souls to discover the world outside and find out what is at the end of the Yellow Brick Road, 'Somewhere over the Rainbow'.

Prospective travellers dream and read about exotic, unpronounceable places. Literature abounds with tempting fictional history. Author-historian Michener tantalises with his versions of how our modern civilisation came about in Hawaii or Jerusalem. Wilbur Smith weaves endless tales of the African continent. Local newspapers produce travel columns about strange lands like Myanmar and Nepal. Colleen McCullough re-creates ancient Rome through the personalities of Julius Caesar and Gallus. These fictional history tales induce dreams of travelling to the far points of our world, where so many cultures and wonders of nature beckon.

Now is the time. Read on, let fantasy become dreams and dreams reality. The saying 'This is the first day of the rest of your life' has never been more to the point.

THE AGE OF MODERN TRAVEL

We of this expiring 20th century have a unique advantage over our parents. The age of air travel makes it possible for us to get to any land of our dreams within a day. The magic carpets of major airlines vie with each other to transport us in varying levels of comfort. A fast train in Japan moves at more than a hundred miles an hour. Slow trains in China cover thousands of miles of history. Modern cruise ships sail the mighty oceans and exotic rivers. Buses and mini vans take groups of travellers and their baggage from place to place in modest comfort with informative guides. Commercial coach lines crisscross territories in reasonable independent comfort. Hire cars are available in almost every part of the world, if you choose to drive yourself. Bicycles can be had for more esoteric touring – or for getting about the locality. Trekkers with or without much endurance or expertise can climb the lower slopes of a mountain or traverse the jungle on marked trails, and find hostels interspersing the routes.

DREAMS CAN COME TRUE

We are talking about you now – the average person turned adventurer, in almost any class of physical condition and most degrees of economic status.

Your dreams are your qualifications, and these can now become realities. Seek out the source of Darjeeling tea by visiting the delightful town of Darjeeling in the mountains of India. Fantasise yourself into the sensual life of Shah Jahan, who built the Taj Mahal in honour of the beloved wife who died in childbirth. Fly to New Delhi, and then on to Agra to stay for a day and a night in the aura of that ancient love. You can, with relative ease, gaze at the pyramids of Egypt or walk on the Great Wall of China – marvels of man's ingenuity.

After the first adrenalin-fed ambitious and adventurous odysseys, the novelty gives way to a wish to enjoy countries or scenes more thoroughly until they are impressed in the memory. Relaxed inveterate travellers, after sating themselves with the wonders of the world and its historic monuments, may elect to rent an apartment in a small town in Switzerland and explore Europe from that base. Britain, France, Italy and the Scandinavian countries are short flights away. For lovers of the sea and beaches, modest locales like the resort-worlds of Port Douglas or Broome, in Australia, offer pleasant havens in which to hunker down and go barefoot. Do for yourself, as the Aussies say, on the barbee, while enjoying an 80-mile beach and the offshore fascinations of the Great Barrier Reef. Go topless with a weird-looking open

Volkswagen Safari, and wander the hinterland at your leisure. Think of the pleasure of staying a month here and a month there, with a freedom so well deserved after a lifetime of work.

Some folk become specialist-venue junkies, desiring to enjoy music in each of the world's opera houses; or to play on every famous golf course, beginning with St Andrews in Scotland; or to follow a gourmet trail; or to stay in the ten best hotels around the globe. Travel magazines tout the newest and finest with hyped up wide-angle-lens pictures enhancing the tiniest of sandy cays. Robin Leach's television travel series depicts the aura of the exclusive, glamorous oases where the Rich and Famous play.

The urge to climb mountains fades as we get older, and we make no apologies for wanting to stay longer in one favourite place. There is comfort in unpacking in a commodious chalet at a pleasant beach resort. Ignore the ins and outs of tour groups, relax under the sun-screening palm trees on expansive lawns. Romantically walk the tidal beach far out into the bay at sunset's low tide. Your chalet becomes a vacation home away from home, complete with maid service and amenities. A choice of restaurants teases your palate and nightclubs your itch to dance. Side trips are enjoyed to a nearby city for shopping, or to the local waterfall or an offshore island to picnic for the day.

Dreams can come true, needing only desire and motivation. Make lists of the myriad wonders of the world to see, odd corners to visit and adventures to undertake – amounting, perhaps, to everything you want to do before your Final Journey. Let *Culture Shock! A Traveller's Guide* tell you how and when.

TIME

An important shock to your travel-culture is the discovery that you have always considered a holiday adventure in terms of two or three weeks. This is ingrained in our society by the international system of workers' holidays. After one year of employment, one week's paid vacation is allowed. Two years bring two weeks. Sometimes long-term employees are offered three weeks of paid holiday. Thus evolved a pattern of two-week trips plus sporting bonuses of stolen weekend days and free national holidays.

Now comes the transition, the real shocker. Suddenly you discover, between jobs, on retirement or with sabbatical leave, that you have months available. A habit of limited travel still brackets the mind. But the children are grown and have flown the nest, pets can be boarded and gardens farmed out. Surprisingly, there is even some extra money in the bank account because daily expenses are less when you are not working. All the old excuses for short-term travel are out of the window. The blinds are lifted, the door is open. Travel time now expands to six weeks or six months.

Excuses

The next thing that happens is the popping up of excuses. "I don't like to live out of a suitcase." "Daughter Sarah's graduation is right in the middle of the time we want to go." Fears, Tremors and Trepidations arise anew (see Chapter Three).

Fear not, excuse not; examine the negatives reasonably, or list them on a tablet. Compare, as with a ledger sheet of assets and liabilities, another column of all the fun places you might visit. List the anticipated joy of not having to cook, make beds or wash windows for a long time. If you find that delectable Shangri-la – a beach resort with everything you've ever wanted at a price you can afford – stay a month. Papa can snorkel to his heart's content, Mama can shop until the credit card overruns. Think about that – and all the negatives won't even tilt the balance sheet.

Beginning

The essence of re-orienting the mind to the new lifestyle is dreaming and planning. We suggest you buy a good world map and hang it near the breakfast table, for a visible and practical start. Begin the adventure. Stick pins in the places you have heard about and find interesting. Make research phone calls, visit the bookshop – and bring home the first instalment of your new life.

The scope is different; start thinking in terms of multiple trips for many years in the future. They take shape on a map, as destinations evolve into a pattern. Singapore, Malaysia and Thailand are together. Fiji and Tahiti are just two of the widely spread Pacific Islands. Hawaii, Alaska and the other United States are in a line if you live in Australia. India, Bhutan and Nepal could make a joint adventure, with Sri Lanka perhaps thrown in if the strife on that fascinating island subsides. Indonesia is a long 'L' from Sumatra to Irian Jaya. China looks like several trips. Make your world list in order of the probable importance of each region to your future plans.

What Time Will Mean
You allow a week for your first destination, and then new thoughts occur. "It would be nice to stay a month on the Costa Azul in Spain while we're on the continent. Portugal is so close, it would be a shame if we didn't drive along the coast and stay in Estoril for a week. Then there is the rest of the Mediterranean, including Corsica and Elba of Napoleonic fame. In Italy, with a day's drive between, are Florence, Rome and Naples. Across the channel is Palermo, in Sicily."

The discussion leads into the matter of how long you can be away. Between two average people this can take many nights of pillow talk and weeks of trying to decide. For extended adventures, no matter what the destination, there is never enough time once you get under way.

For those still committed to a career, on a mere three weeks holiday from work, be sure to stretch the time off to include a TGIF Friday, and talk the boss into your return on a Tuesday morning. That adds up to 24 days instead of 21 – neatly offsetting the days lost in international transit. Don't waste one of the extra days to pack your bags or close up the house. Plan ahead and do all the chores beforehand.

Book your travel tickets to leave as early as possible and return as late as possible.

In the following year, build up credits, angle for a four-week holiday by compromising on something during the year. Think aerobically, add a week each year by hook or crook. Soon you will be retired – and will already have accustomed yourself to lengthy travel.

TIMING

Proper timing is the key to successful and enjoyable travelling. Weather factors have to be included in the formula as you really won't like Melbourne in the southern winter of June, July and August. Beijing in January is miserable unless you love to wear thermal underwear and sniffle for days on end. Still in the work force? Dependent on scheduled holidays? Then pick the best destination for now and keep the others on a back burner for when you do have the privilege of selecting your own time.

School holidays or the annual *haj* of thousands to Mecca can suddenly upset a requested reservation on Malaysian Airlines. China's trade fairs in Guangzhou fill up Hong Kong's hotels in the spring and autumn. You don't want to be caught in the typhoon season in the middle of a Pacific cruise. These facts crop up when you begin talking to airlines and other travel people during the planning stage. Mark down any and all information regarding the right or wrong time to go, for future reference.

The space flight planners call this system 'Windows'. A window is the preferred or necessary space of time to take off and land. Create your own windows, when you list a destination, by marking a calendar with the ideal and near ideal times to travel there. Keep accumulating data to add to your Timing Calendar. A travel article may suggest the perfect occasion to visit because of a Mardi Gras festival or the Dragon Boat races or Chinese New Year. Once addicted to the thrill of travelling, you will have many years in which to visit the desired adventure spot at the optimum time.

Social Events

Family dates have to be added to your travel calendar as far in advance as possible: a wedding in the offing, a favourite niece's graduation from college or the bash of the year at your best friend's home. Knowledge in advance will allow you to work around those dates or find some way to weasel out of the obligation for a greater purpose. Somehow, being selfish in these matters has never been a negative word. It translates into personal happiness and comparing the joy of a wonderful adventure to missing a party.

Illness

Accidents and illness create the worst difficulties. If you or your travelling companion suddenly develop a problem that needs immediate attention, then you will have to change your plans. The serious illness of a close friend or relative poses a more awkward problem. Analyse it. You may conclude that, having made your splendid gesture, you could not do much that was helpful – and that all parties would be happier on your return if you went ahead with your plans.

Chapter Two

RETIRED AND ADVENTUROUS

TRIGG.

Newly-retired people are all for travel, now that they have the time. The desire is there; and then well-meaning friends and relatives become scoffers. They say, "You've worked hard all your life. You can rest now. Stay at home, enjoy your retirement and save your money for old age." The naysayers point out every article in the papers about plane crashes in China, tourists being killed in Miami, and Harrods being bombed in London – and then ask, "What if the arthritis acts up again?"

No cause for debate: it is your life and your decision. Enjoy the new chapter in your story. Do what you want. I equate the unfriendly word 'retire' with a new facet to my career – almost a reincarnation. You may choose to sit in your rocking chair, become an orchid fancier, grow peanuts ... *or* don wings and fly off into the wild blue yonder. Statistics show that occasional flying is a thousand times safer than driving to work every day; and a few days of beach and warm sun do wonders for aches and pains. Read the next chapter to rationalise all the worries. Look forward to the fun and adventure you'll have. Tell the friends and relatives, nicely, to buzz off and let you enjoy the rest of your life.

DO IT NOW

Retirement is a shifting-of-gears life change. Some indeed retire into the proverbial rocking chair, sit on the porch, worry about money and wait for the end to come. Others have planned and dreamed of what they want to do in the future. If you have travelled, on limited two- or three-week annual vacations, now is the moment to take a real trip. For the first time in your life, you can leave home for one or two months. Ask a neighbour to water the plants and feed the pets.

Explore the land of your dreams leisurely at its best time of year, avoiding bad weather and the edges of high seasons. Escape the crowds and miss the stiffer prices. Climb your desired mountain slowly, in physical comfort. Take a train across a continent, stopping en route for interesting interludes. Allow months, not weeks, to see in a relaxed manner the places you have dreamt about. Stay for a week at each ancient site instead of the meaningless one-night stand. Laze around in 'Deluxe Economy' comfort at an inexpensive resort, not worrying about cooking meals, doing the laundry or making the beds. It's nice being waited on for a few weeks, while indulging in the new sport of extended travelling. A fresh plateau of your life beckons, promising adventure and tingling the spine, like joining a Star Trek craft into outer space.

You will return home to the wonderment of family and friends, looking years younger, tanned, trim, dressed in bright new clothes and minus facial pouches. Then show off the photos or video tapes of your escapades and adventures, and brag about planning an even longer trip next year.

The average person has spent 20 years maturing and 40 years working – and now deserves another 40-plus to travel around and have fun before counting as old.

NEW OUTLOOK

A residual advantage of travelling at this change-of-life stage is the proverbial new outlook, fresh start attitude. Yes, wandering does broaden the mind, extend horizons, re-generate ambitions and relax inhibitions. New careers are often conceived when visiting other parts of the world, meeting new people, developing ideas that may have lain dormant for many years.

Societies, nations, vehicles, and environments are changing rapidly. Closeted in our own country and home, we have hardly noticed these stepless changes. The age of electronics is a sleeping giant ready to engulf our lives. Easy air travel extends into the tiniest island and remotest area. When you get out of your own cocoon and travel with other people – adventurers like yourself – the exchange of ideas stimulates. You receive a stimulus to look around, obtain a new outlook and do something about it.

New horizons can take in another career. Assuming you have a retirement income, and some savings for security, you are not now trying to make a fortune. A fresh idea will be good in itself; and all the better if it adds to your income and so increases your opportunities to indulge in leisure and pleasure.

An interest in boats may develop into a cruise and holiday-fishing business in a beautiful harbour city, and produce enough revenue in three or four months of high-season work to pay for the upkeep of a magnificent sailing yacht – which will serve your own pleasure for the rest of the year. A cottage acquired by the seashore or up in a mountain resort area can be turned into a

Bed-and-Breakfast place, and provide a modest additional income. Your local newspaper may be keen to pay for personal interest travel articles: camera, laptop computer and baby-printer are all the equipment needed. Artistic hobbies, like painting or collecting antiques, develop into travel incentives and then perhaps begin to generate income. Such are the opportunities discovered while adventuring around the world.

DISAGREEMENT

Face it, put the facts on the table, and consider the downside. Two people, married happily for a quarter of a century, are suddenly confronted with freedom of choice – and become incompatible. Perhaps the man had a long and physically or mentally tiring career and wants to play golf or tennis, grow radishes and relax with cronies and a beer every afternoon. The lady of the house is looking forward to getting out of her home-workplace and away from the chores of making beds, cooking, washing windows and raising grandchildren.

Impasse? Travel can solve the problem if looked at in the light of a compromise solution. We suggest alternative ideas and open minds. A woman can travel safely and enjoyably in a small group or paired with a like-minded friend (see Chapters Nine and Ten), leaving the husband in his sedentary comfort with a fridge full of frozen dinners. It's not the end of their marriage or relationship, merely a new-found freedom to be enjoyed by both parties. In modern society there is every reason to change the tactics to prolong the game.

Another problem arises when the partners agree to travel but have different destinations in mind. Compromise is then in order. Let both lay their cards on the table and play the hand. Take a notebook and, under separate thee and me headings, list each other's ace destination idea – followed by a second and a third choice. Under each listed area, enter the probable activities there. A pattern develops, inevitably. Beach and sunshine pop up regularly on both sides of the page. Golf courses and fishing opportunities appear along with jungle treks and the viewing of ancient temples. Of 20 potential activities, 16 turn up under both parties' names. Not so bad, eh? Twenty per cent can easily be sorted out by common sense and compromise.

Plan several itineraries: the current trip and the next few years' adventures.

She will give up her night markets and beach hotel for two weeks, in favour of his yachting expedition. He will surrender golf in view of her yearning to see Nepal, where there are no golf courses. Surprisingly, human nature makes the yield better than expected. For many people find themselves disagreeing almost for the sake of doing so, in a spirit of stubborn refusal to see the other person's viewpoint. There is an old remedy: think of *how* you can do it and not *why* you can't.

Sometimes it dawns on people who have lived together all their adult lives that a couple of weeks away from each other will not cause disaster. It's a welcome change to have a wee bit of independence, a break from routine. He can go one way to play golf, take lunch and beer with the boys and maybe try a poker game. The telly can show sports broadcasts and rebroadcasts until he falls asleep in the chair. She at last can see the pyramids of Egypt, cruise down the Nile and shop in legendary bazaars. When the twain meet after a fortnight or two, romance buds anew, following the axiom 'Absence makes the heart grow fonder'.

"Go West young man," Horace Greely, an early American publisher and journalist, once advised. His meaning was: explore a new world, create a fresh start, opportunity is ripe on the tree. 'West' is symbolic of a new direction, and 'young' of your age as you see it. Thus explained, the advice is as good today as it was a hundred years ago.

The chapters that follow define in detail how to interpret that advice, and so create a wonderful future of travelling. Each section encourages you to research and find out for yourself the best way to enjoy your new lifestyle. Your destinations and activities change; hotels grow stale and you replace them with newer or older ones. The tourist's atlas is continually changing. Travel agents, airlines, modes of transport are in flux. We suggest how to travel confidently in our preferred status of 'Deluxe Economy' – which we define as the best possible accommodation at the best possible price.

It is never too late for adventure and pleasure.

Chapter Three

FEARS, TREMORS AND TREPIDATIONS

Fear of the unknown is typical amongst inexperienced travellers, especially in the case of a first adventure or a woman touring alone. Anticipated language barriers – plus world news of plane crashes, crime and riots – top the list. Next come worries about hygiene and personal health. Then concern about being away from family and home for extended periods. These mental aberrations eventually soften with experience, when the traveller realizes that the world of adventure is comfortable and home doesn't change much in a month or two.

Regardless of age, most people's ingrained desire for adventure is in conflict with those trepidations. The potential stalemate can be overcome by taking things slowly at first. Buy a well-run tour package that takes care of the travel details (see *Travel Agent – Friend or Foe?* in Chapter Four). You can then enjoy sightseeing, shopping, people and fellow-travellers without worrying about minor questions. On the next trip, spread the wings and soar out on your own – after which you will believe that luggage does not get lost most of the time, schedules are reasonably kept to, hotels honour reservations, and menus are in English.

My wife will often worry about enough hot water for her morning shower, while I fret over getting an extension of a few days at a particularly wonderful resort hotel we have stumbled upon. All such worries are trivial compared with the overall enjoyment of being in another part of the world, free as a seagull in the land of your dreams.

Well, here you are. The plane took off and landed on time, with your luggage. Hotel Super-Duper had your reservation and ensconced you in a beautiful room overlooking the ocean. A bowl of local fruit and a bottle of champagne are on the table, welcoming you to the Seventh Heaven. On the desk are brochures and information about all the remarkable things you can see and do during your stay. Thrills tingle the spine in anticipation of weeks of pleasure, adventure, interesting foods and the luxury of being taken care of.

FEAR OF FLYING

Fear of flying is the most common trembler, even for those who have flown dozens of times. The persistent and gruesome television coverage of some light plane that crashed in Timbuktu, with no survivors, dominates the evening news. The media choose to feature air crashes around the world as important information, even when they involve only a few people in a remote region on a small airline unfamiliar to the home audience. Not so with the half-dozen tragedies that occur on the roads of a nearby city every day, unless they involve a famous person.

Major air crashes, of the kind that happen once or twice a year, are heavily covered worldwide; the pictures made of them are shown again and again from the library of films.

Strangely (perhaps), only airline advertisements report the many safe flights completed each day to and from the destinations you have in mind. Can you imagine the news value of this television announcement: "Today's 72 flights between Tokyo and Los Angeles or Singapore all arrived safely and within time schedules. Some 21,600 passengers boarded, ate 64,200 meals and watched 144 films. Moreover, all 63,200 pieces of luggage were restored to their owners on arrival."? No news value there, but think about it.

The huge Boeing 747 you are booked on has a legendary record as the safest large plane in history. The chances of being injured or killed within a short radius of your own home, as against air travel of any kind, are millions to one. Think of every hour in the air as being safe from a local traffic accident.

Serious airsickness, though seldom occurring in large aircraft, is alleviated by doctor-advised pills or patches behind the ear. If you haven't been troubled by the problem before, don't worry about it.

First timers, and those who travel a lot and still tremble when strapped into the seat, can assuage their fear. Arrive early at the airport: at least an hour before the required time. This saves check-in queuing and gives time to have a post-check-in snack and watch the hundreds of other passengers, in peace. Actually being amid the excitement of other air travellers – business people, families, old or handicapped folk, and youthful backpackers – gives the assurance of safety in numbers. Major airports can be pleasant places with shops and restaurants, plus views of the landing field and aircraft taxiing. Arrive early, then, relax in a pub or cafeteria, change some money into the next country's currency. A good adventure novel or an intriguing crossword puzzle makes a soothing balm for pre-flight nerves.

Relieve yourself – ready or not – before boarding the plane. That means before entering your flight's numbered departure 'lounge'. To get up, stand in a queue when airborne, and use the tiny closet they call a toilet, is an unpleasant chore for a worried flyer. You feel and actually are safer, buckled into your armchair until you have landed – except for moments of leg-stretching.

In flight, read, watch the film, do another crossword puzzle or listen to programmes with the headphones. Snack but don't eat heavily. Liquor is far more upsetting than soothing in the oxygenated atmosphere at 35,000 feet above sea level. The odds are that the plane will bounce several times during a long flight. This is caused by air pockets.

Keep the seatbelt fastened at all times when you are seated. Never mind what the loudspeaker says about freedom to move about the cabin, or what your seat neighbour does.

Noises of the aircraft on take-off and landing are disturbing if you are not familiar with them. Engines are revved up or down, changing the drone of in-flight operation. Wheels and other gadgets go clunk and thump. This is the crew operating the machinery, not engines falling off. Settle down; the noises are comforting, evidence of someone flying the craft that is taking you to your destination.

Put the seat back, remove your shoes, tuck a pillow under your head or in the middle of your back; wrap a blanket round you if the air-conditioning is cold, taking special care of your feet. Try to nap, or daydream about the first full day after your arrival. It makes the time pass quickly and lulls the heartbeat.

Self-hypnosis

A family doctor once counselled me on how to take short naps when working hard or under stress. It is very effective on any long journey. Close your eyes and imagine yourself in peaceful familiar surroundings, whether of beach, woodland or neighbourhood. 'Walk' slowly, creating a mental image – in great detail – with each step. Picture precisely each recollection: bush, tree, stone, bird, animal, wind-movement or wave. It's a form of self-hypnosis, and it can work wonders. Practise the identical scene, whether flying, trying to nap, or going to sleep at night. Repetition of this one sequence is the key to the door of relief. Even a brief ten minutes will slow down the whole spinning world to the speed of your idling body. You wake surprisingly refreshed. When it coincides with your normal time for sleeping, this 'hypnosis' should induce a longer natural sleep.

If you are reading a book, then to fall asleep, re-read the same page over and over and over again until the words blur and the eyes naturally close. Most passengers plug in the earphones to watch the movies or let music lull them. We prefer to dissociate ourselves from the in-house entertainment while flying. Trying to concentrate on the film while the person in front keeps moving is disconcerting. Speaker sound is notoriously poor in aircraft. If you enjoy good music while travelling, bring your own small battery-powered tape- or disc-player(s) with private earphones; you will enjoy them much more.

All of this advice is to transmute the fear of flying into a modicum of comfort by lulling the senses until the plane lands. In Chapter Eight, *Transport by Air* covers the jet-lag problem and endorses the theory of special exercises en route.

WHAT IF I FALL ILL OR HAVE AN ACCIDENT?

Chapters Thirteen and Fourteen give details, with specific instances and answers. For the moment we shall deal with the general question of illness while away, or being treated by an unknown foreign doctor. Your own physician knows your health background, your idiosyncrasies and what to do when your stomach acts up. "But what does this doctor know about me?"

I respond to such fears, and to the rest of the "what if's?" in the same lump-in-your-throat category, with a simplified answer: "Do the same as you would at home". If you get a cold, slurp bowls of noodle soup, drink pots of tea with lemon and honey, and sweat it out with bed rest. If the cold persists or serious dysentery takes over, see a local doctor; one is always, repeat always, available wherever you go. Except at the top of Mount Everest or the source of the Amazon, I assure you that medical facilities are accessible. The local doctor knows what flu bug is around, and the proper antibiotic to counteract it. If you are a real worrier there is nothing more I can say to help. A fatalist merely adds "*Que sera, sera*; whatever will be, will be."

Worrier or not, don't forget to read Chapters Thirteen and Fourteen, or to pack the information therein described, which would put a local doctor in touch with your records and – if need be – with your physician.

The key to calm and sensible travel is – be prepared.

PHOBIAS

A phobia is defined as an unnatural fear or great dislike of something. Mine is of heights, like climbing a ladder or getting into those glass elevators. My wife fears deep water and gets jumpy about strange noises. Phobias are easier to handle in a crowd – safety in numbers again. If it's hygiene and the table-ware, be continental and boldly wipe the things down with your napkin, and damn the snide look from the waiter. Consider any serious phobias before you leave, in the planning process.

People have phobias about small aeroplanes or boats, for example; and out of the way retreats often entail a feeder-airline and an hour-long boat ride in a choppy sea. Investigate, try to contact a traveller who has been there recently, to find out the exact situation. Selling agents obviously play down or ignore such problems.

A sudden confrontation with your worst fears can be very unsettling in a foreign country.

Pre-planning and information will ease matters. Admittedly, the problems will not disappear. But facing the anxiety head on, and discussing it with a friend or probable travelling companion, goes a long way towards alleviating the phobia or putting it in proper proportion.

Personal Experience
In New Zealand, we bought an air-travel pass with Mount Cook Airlines to tour the North and South Islands. Turbulent air and small planes are phobias of my wife and myself. The sales staff assured us that all flights in New Zealand were short and September weather was mild. After one particularly upsetting half-hour flight from Auckland to the Bay of Islands, we gave up the pass (no refund) and rented a car. The pilot couldn't understand our discomfort, as he flew the route every day with no qualms. Another facet of this experience was our discovery of the right way to travel in New Zealand. Except for moving between the two islands, driving is much the better way to enjoy the land of milk and honey and the Kiwi. Roads are pleasant, distances short and the small towns delightful.

☛ **Lesson Learned**
Don't stick with a bad situation because of pre-purchased tickets. Your comfort is more important.

TRUST THYSELF
Distrust is a phobia, often the result of a bad experience at some point in life. Money is one of the most vexing problems. It is human nature to wonder: "What if I lose my wallet? What if the taxi driver is going to take us the long way round and overcharge? What will happen if I don't tip the waiter or the porter? Am I getting the right exchange rate for my money?" My daugh-

ter used to ask, when we were travelling in Mexico, "How much is this in real money Dad?" Foreign currency often affects one as if it were Monopoly money.

Another common phobia is distrust that human beings will do what they said they would. Your guide arranged to pick you up at 9:00 and it's already 9:02 and she isn't there yet. "Oh my God, we'll miss the plane." Or, in the "what if?" category, suppose our neighbour forgets to water the petunias?

Control your fears as best you can by taking the specific precautions described elsewhere in this book. A general Pollyanna answer is "Relax and don't let paranoia overcome the enjoyment of your trip." Yes, there are people out to get the unwary; and an honest mistake can be made by others in charge of your adventure. A porter or waiter may sneer at you behind your back for not leaving a tip when they gave poor service. So what? Guides cause themselves all kinds of trouble by being too late, often after arranging an extra-early pick-up time for their own convenience.

The point is: trust thyself to know what to do in these instances. Worry, if you must, about anything and everything. But not to distraction. Life is too short.

LEAVING HOME

Three- to six-week adventures are not too severe on the routines of home life. Two- to six-month holidays require more sophisticated plans. The first time is the hardest because you remember all the things you should have done after you leave: too late. A written list prepared far in advance is important. Feed the pets... water the plants... cancel the monthly whist game or group social... clean out the perishables from the refrigerator... pay actual and foreseeable bills... stop the newspaper, the milk...

Leave Word of Where You'll Be

Travel agents provide the itinerary for the services you book.

Ask them to add addresses plus fax and telephone numbers of the major hotels, etc., as contact and mailing points for relations, friends and firms. Independent travellers will prepare their own itinerary and have these numbers readily available. Leave a copy of your intended route, dates and addresses with the family member or neighbour who will handle your mail and forward important items to you. Except in very remote places, airmail will take from four to ten days; it is generally reliable. For urgent matters, such international forwarders as Federal Express, United Parcel Service and DHL guarantee express delivery within 48 to 72 hours.

If you change your plans midway, do pass this news back.

FINANCIAL AFFAIRS

Your friendly bank manager can arrange to pay current bills, mortgages, utilities and even your credit card balance, from your basic account. Overdraft arrangements are quite common for known clients. It's best to leave the bank a copy of your itinerary, in case someone wants to deposit a million dollars in your account and the manager needs your investment advice.

WOOFers (Well Off Over Forties) with sophisticated financial affairs obviously have to make suitable arrangements with stockbrokers, bankers and legal advisors. It is common to give a *limited power of attorney* to a close member of the family, to be used in case of communication problems. Let me emphasise: with modern telephone, fax and air parcel facilities, most emergencies are easily handled.

Worry not, fret not, tremble not – enjoy, instead!

Chapter Four

CHOOSING A TOUR PACKAGE

You start your exciting adventure plans by choosing a tour package or selecting an independent holiday. The process absorbs your interest as you seek the location of your dreams. Finding the proper package of transport, accommodation and associated services is of key importance. The financial expenditure is significant; the time you invest may be more so – if it is the only chance to get away during a whole year. Anticipation of the fun and exhilaration of adventure is part of the planning process. A wonderful experience creates a desire to repeat it again and again. Poor episodes can easily sour the mood for extensive travelling in the future, reflected in the expression "what do I need this trouble for?"

It is very important therefore that you do considerable research into the intended travel area; carefully select the travel bureau and agent; compare tours and understand the system.

TOUR RESEARCH

Regardless of any friendship or supposed obligation to an agent, research the travel area yourself before visiting a professional. All major destination countries have friendly overseas offices, anxious to attract you, the money-spending tourist. Look in the *Yellow Pages* under 'Tourist information' or, if unsuccessful, try the listings under 'Embassies, Consulates and Legations'. People living far from an urban centre can call a city's Directory Enquiry service. A few coins spent on telephone calls at the outset can save you hundreds later. The immediate reward is the packets of data and brochures they cheerfully send you, to answer questions and stir up further excitement.

The first travel agency on record was established by Thomas Cook of Leicester in England in 1841, with branches gradually added around the world; now they are one of many chains. Personal visits and telephone enquiries to major international travel bureaux such as Thomas Cook and American Express will yield specific tour pamphlets before you feel committed to one of them. This first flood of information is only the beginning.

Travel Guides and Reference Books

Investigate bookshops that specialise in or at least have a full shelf of travel guides and related material such as the *Culture Shock!* series. A friendly salesperson can consult a computer for other items, available on order. You may have to look further than your favourite shopping complex. Do some more *Yellow Pages* phone reference work to find at least two shops that sound intelligent and knowledgeable. Those of us who left school many years ago tend to forget the public libraries. For instance, if you want to find out more about the animal kingdom in Africa to back up your intended tour, take time to research the library.

When you have acquired some background, the next step is to gather price information and draw up a budget. Consult the travel bureau that seems most considerate and relevant to your needs. If you detect misinformation or a pushy clod, take your leave and go to another.

TRAVEL AGENT – FRIEND OR FOE?

Of paramount importance is finding the right travel bureau and within it a specific agent or employee to *negotiate* your plans. A travel agency and its representatives are brokers between you and the providers of accommodation and long- and short-haul transport. The representative's job is to arrange a travel programme between you and those various vendors. The agent is supposedly representing your best interests, but commission agents earn their fees from their bookings. In legal parlance, this is a conflict of interest; therefore suspect the worst until proven otherwise.

Conscientious travel bureaux know that their best interests are served if you return year after year as a valued client. A positive approach sets the stage and states your new-found interest in travel. "We are looking for a good agency to help us arrange all of our travelling in the future. Please tell me something about your firm." The attitude and response will be very revealing, since the question is unexpected. If the response is "Where do you want to go?", you are not off to a good start. While most clients approach the firm with a request for specific travel arrangements, you are interested in the quality and methods of the agency first.

☛ **Travel Tip**
On entering a large travel office for the first time, look around, watch the traffic, observe the senior agents (often in glassed-in offices). It is usually possible to spot the

supervisors giving directions to others. Pick up a name from a desk plate, or ask directly for the senior agent. Offer a business card, introduce yourself as someone (perhaps important) seeking a reliable agency to arrange not just this one trip but years of future travel. You (as it happens) *are* important. Even if you are passed on to another agent, you are sure to get VIP attention instead of the treatment accorded to one who casually drops in.

The whole task is by no means easy. Singapore's *Yellow Pages*, for instance, prints 14 pages of Travel Bureaux. Phoenix, Arizona, has 10 pages, with over a hundred firms to choose from. You may have a friend or a friend's friend in the travel business. Take care; that happy chance could result in a spoiled trip and an ex-friend.

Choose wisely. Look for proficiency, demeanour and evidence of experience. The travel bureau and its staff are important factors in your proposed adventures. You desire the best value for your money and they are selling merchandise on a commission; different objectives. Even the celebrated Thomas Cook's and American Express employ personnel called agents to sell their products. The more the agents sell, the more their income: a lurking threat to your long-awaited adventure. Until you begin negotiating with them, you have no real idea of their expertise or their priorities.

The ideal agency is owner-operated, experienced in the business for many years, and the widely-travelled proprietor is there to supervise or handle your programme personally.

"Travel is cheaper by the dozen and with double occupancy." So saith the travel industry. Not always true – but 'Independent Travel' is the subject of the next chapter. Here we shall note the agencies' hype, and examine the where and how of the tour package. Asking the right questions to find out whether your agent is a friend or a foe is the key to enjoyable travelling.

Bypass the holiday weekend ads and look for the extended

tours. The standard brochure dealing with your destination will list package tours from 7 to 21 days. A map indicates the various routes from the arrival city. Your own research has given you an overview of the country, its size and principal points of interest.

Board Terms
American Plan means with a substantial breakfast. Half Board includes dinner also. Full Board means all meals included. If there is nowhere else to dine, you will probably get the best deal with Full Board. Lunch is immaterial but dinner at night is important. If there are alternative restaurants, it's more fun to go out on your own and enjoy a variety of dinners – and even snack lunches. Always ask how much it would be without the meals, to give you a comparison. If you are a coffee-and-toast breakfast eater, the morning buffet/American Breakfast is a waste of money. *A la carte* gives you full freedom of choice: whether to take (and pay for) the meal – and which items to take.

QUESTIONS TO TEST AGENCY'S COMPETENCE
- When were you last there?
- Is the flight non-stop, and how long does it take?
- What is the time change on arrival?
- If there is a choice of hotels, what are the differences?
- What do 'Superior', 'Deluxe' and 'Standard' mean there?
- Is the hotel in town or out of the way?
- Tell me about the side trips.
- Should we book them after arrival?
- Does the journey there involve small planes or boats?
- How much unescorted shopping time will we have?
- What is the weather like during the selected period?
- Specify the meals included.
- How many people will be on the same tour with us?
- Where do others in the group come from?
- Are children allowed?

- If coastal, is there beach swimming, snorkeling, etc.?
- When are the shark and stinger seasons?
- Is special equipment or clothing suggested?

Where and when to book side trips or day excursions is the sting question. Avaricious agents want to add everything they can to the itinerary. It is much better to arrange local tours on site.

☛ **Travel Tip**
Be efficient. Bring a note pad. Write the questions out beforehand; record the answers, and everything else including your opinion of the tour offered and the agent. Otherwise, after visiting three different travel bureaux, it would be impossible to remember which offered what.

Take the questions and answers seriously. A five-star hotel may be overwhelmed with problems, dulling its gleam. A reliable 50- or 100-room hotel in London will be far more personal than a 500-room one, if you are booked in for a week or more. Daily scenic side trips can be miserable if you are going to spend most of each day on a smelly bus or in a small boat in rough waters. Your previously-purchased guide book lists hotels and miscellaneous information (see Chapter Six). If you get answers that appear to contradict the guide book, ask specific questions such as "Why the Baywatch Hotel instead of the more important and newer Seaside Sheraton?" Package deals often have direct tie-ins with bargain based units, for the convenience and advantage of the packager; these units do not always give you your best value.

Shopping and Free Time
These are particularly important. Some tours are timed for the bus to stop for 15 minutes, and then the whistle blows to get back on board. Others are geared to prolong a tawdry shopping

opportunity beyond reason. The most desirable is an afternoon at leisure to browse through a market (or temple-cum-market) without guides or timetable.

Full Board

Having meals included (other than breakfast) is a deterrent to exploring unusual local restaurants. This becomes significant if you stay for more than a day or two in one place. The group gathers at breakfast and dinner every day of the trip because it is included, meaning you have already paid for it. But think: you have travelled thousands of miles to be here, investing a great deal of money in order to see, taste and have fun in a famous city or a picturesque town; and your guide book lists a particularly fine seafood restaurant on the wharf. Throw away your dinner coupon, separate from the travel group, get a taxi and take off by yourselves. This is the spirit of adventure travel, and it will leave in your memory the better taste.

Comments on Some of the Other Questions

Weather is unpredictable at best, but the general highs and lows for each month are available. Ask, even if you already know the answer, to see if the agent is alert. Major newspapers carry daily world-wide weather reports, but you have to monitor them for some time if you want useful information.

What companions to expect in your travel party? A mixed nationality group is very interesting to some travellers, but inhibiting to others. Small children can be discomfiting to tourists looking for a change from such company.

Many beach resorts have magnificent ocean-front locations, but are impossible for swimming because of tides, rocks, sharks, unhealthy waters, or seasonally dangerous jellyfish. It is very disappointing to go there for sun, sea and surf, and find that only the sun can be enjoyed, or that you have arrived in the monsoon season when it is only the rain that you can soak in. Ask specifically, if you enjoy ocean swimming, about the beach and water conditions.

If, when you get there, you see a buoyed rope marking a safe-to-swim area, make sure that the net which the rope is supposed to support is there too.

The important key to the 'Friend or foe' question is: "Was the agent listening to and answering queries, or avoiding them?" An experienced agent is well travelled and well read. "I will find out for you, madam" is better than an intelligent guess.

COMPARING TOURS

To compare the value of various tours offered, use this simple formula. Count the days lost in transit from home to hotel, and from one area to another. Subtract these lost days from the total and divide the balance into the full cost of the trip. For example, a 21-day tour loses one day from home to Africa, and another on the return. The itinerary details one day each in changing from South Africa to Zimbabwe, thence to Kenya and so on, leaving 16 days available to enjoy the holiday areas of the tour. The value of your trip is 16, not 21, days.

Compare costs of different tours offered, by dividing the residual days into the package total. Well-planned tours have a minimum amount of wasted travel time. When you see the hype of 'Eight days and seven nights in tropical splendour', translate that as a six-day vacation. 'Three days and two nights' boils down to "How many hours will we actually have on the beach?"

Flight schedules are important. When you get to talking about the precise details of a particular tour, pay attention to the time of each flight and whether there is any choice. Late after-noon and evening flight departures incur a miserable lost day of waiting around with little to do. When there is no choice, at least you know what you are in for and you will look for something interesting to fill the void when you get there. Good planning will include places to see, or a local side trip to fill the lost hours.

Bad planning says queue up and wait. If there is no choice on your part, being forewarned gives the opportunity to select another tour.

☛ **Travel Tip**

Do read the contract, including the small print, thoroughly *before signing*. The if's, and's and but's are explicit about what contractual rights you have. Changes are never allowed, so don't accept an assurance from an aggressive agent that some item can be disregarded. Cancellation-and-money-back rules are the most important feature.

THE SYSTEM

The commercial system of the travel industry creates a wholesaler, and a retail travel bureau. Larger companies (wholesalers) organise specific tours, arrange for reduced fees from guaranteed space on airlines and hotels, and add a profit. Smaller agencies (retailers) pre-book packages to sell on. Though there is seldom a price difference, try to use the source (the wholesaler). Book with them direct because they will have the best up-to-date information. Originators are usually identified in the package pamphlet as (for example) Singapore Airlines' subsidiary Silk Air or the Qantas subsidiary, Jetabout. The originator will also have on hand plans for the next selling season, which may be when you are planning to go.

In summary, you wouldn't pay hundreds for new furnishings in the parlour without shopping around. Take time, use the same good judgement, and shop for your travel adventure. Find the right Friend and you won't have to fend off a Foe.

☛ **Personal Experience**

From New Delhi, the capital of India, our pre-booked itinerary included the customary day trip to Agra to visit the famous Taj Mahal. It consisted of three hours in an almost broken down bus, a miserable two-hour lunch stop, one hour at the Taj Mahal, another at the Red Fort, and three hours back in the heat, smog and slow traffic. In a 10-hour trip, our actual viewing time was no more than two hours. Caution: in any foreign country, don't take the travel desk's word for anything. Ask some returning tourists who took the same trip the previous day. Angry and disappointed customers are quick and frank to point out the problems and alternatives. In this case, we would have been better off discarding the pre-booked and prepaid side trip. We discovered later that the ideal way to see Agra is to fly in and stay overnight in the excellent hotel there. We could thus have enjoyed the Taj Mahal at and before sunset and sunrise for hours, when most of the tour buses and their thousands of people were absent.

Chapter Five

THE INDEPENDENT
TRAVELLER

Dawn is breaking, your plane lands at the faraway airport. Chattering excitement builds around you as everyone gathers carry-on baggage. You leave the aircraft to arrive in a new world on the first day of your travel adventure. Formalities are completed in quick order and the luggage appears on the luggage belt. Thrilling sensations take over as the taxi takes you to the impressive five-star hotel in a strange city, or an arranged guide whisks you away to a thatched hut on a remote beach. Arrival is romantic, fascinating, pregnant with rare experiences and adventures. And… you did it all yourself.

There is an extra thrill in independent travelling. It is the freedom of arriving at your destination without a prescribed schedule. Time is your own. Tour the city, take a side trip, go shopping, stay a week or more if you like. Weary, now, from time and nervous energy expended during the last 24 hours of travelling? Take a day to relax by the pool, read the local brochures, talk to the nice people next to you about where they have been. No rush. You have plenty of time to soothe the frazzled nerves and plan the rest of your odyssey.

The Beginning

As with Chapter Four's tour package, decide on your area of destination: the Orient, Europe, Africa, the Middle East, South or North America, or the South Pacific. Follow the previous research suggestions: they are even more important if you are going to travel independently. Enquire for the air travel packages of the airlines which fly direct to your chosen destination. For really long air journeys, ask about Circle Pacific (CP) or Around the World Tickets (AWT) and similar combinations. When no airline covers your intended adventure completely, you might strike a bargain with two carriers in combination to give an all-encompassing fare. Increasingly, airlines are forming alliances which make bargains of this kind before you ask.

There is advanced planning to be done, with research; special air fares and travel packages will be discovered. This can be part of the fun for those adventurous self-confident souls who value the distinction of travelling at their own pace.

NON-SCHEDULED INDEPENDENCE

One method of Independent Travel is to select the destination area; and book the there-and-back flight and the first hotel, only. Then, free as air, you proceed to arrange the scenic strategy from day to day as the weather, local information and your moods suggest. To some, this may sound alarming or inhibiting. Others revel in the adventure of such freedom.

Time is important. On a three-day weekend you are more

likely to hunker down in the city, hotel or beach resort, see the local sights and relax by the pool. But on a three-week holiday, there is time enough to explore the country, take side trips to neighbouring scenic wonders, tour the museums or explode in a frenzy of shopping. Three months permit extensive travel over a range of territory – or a starfish pattern of intensive exploration from a central base.

The travel industry records a growing trend of people wanting to go out and see the world, *sans* schedule, and doing without greeters and meeters, precise reservations or pre-planned side tours. Until recently, this was mainly the device of back-packers, young independents travelling thither and yon for five dollars a day, hitching rides and bunking in hostels. At the other extreme were the wealthy, travelling first class, with entourage, by air and sea, being met by stretch limousines, and ending the day in presidential suites.

Now we, the great middle class and middle aged (from 40 to 80 plus), rise up to find our place in the sun, literally. The travel industry secretly calls us WOOFers (Well Off Old Folk, or Well Off Over Forties) in their plans to sell us tours. We, the Independent Woofers, have sufficient funds to travel in comfort and we shun the structured programme. I term the style of travel we like, Deluxe Economy.

We have a yen to rent a vehicle and self-drive around a country, stop at a series of interesting inns or stay put to visit the caves and waterfalls in some fascinating locale. Domestic airlines in most countries can shuffle us around with little advance notice. Many top-rated holiday areas have space available at the last minute, though not during a school holiday or when a convention has booked them solid for the weekend. However, we, the independent flexible travellers, can go on a Tuesday or a Thursday, take the morning or afternoon plane and adapt easily to whatever occurs.

The strategy is to book the overseas journey and the first

hotel. Research has netted a thick file of what to do and where to go during our stay. We have a tentative list of the more important scenic wonders and of nearby areas to visit; and we have practised how to say hello, goodbye and thank you in the local vernacular.

To set up our non-scheduled independent non-programme, we may elect to book the reservations directly or have a knowledgeable travel agency do the booking. I make the airline reservations myself, but ask the agency to write the tickets as a matter of convenience. Hotels are booked direct.

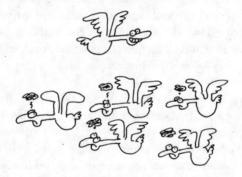

SCHEDULED INDEPENDENTS

On the other hand there is something to be said for a well-planned adventure, fitting into a general timetable with advance reservations. This is necessary when the allotted time is short. It is comforting to know that a guide or hotel car will meet you on arrival at each air- or seaport with satisfying efficiency. You have a pre-arranged schedule, theatre tickets have been booked, the side trip to the nearby mountain resort is confirmed – and will begin in the morning.

Travel agents advise that this will cost more than a packaged group tour. In practice they build a package with prices quoted by airline, hotel for room and meals, plus greeting and guide services. The total price, including commission/profit margin, is take-it-or-leave-it for the buyer. Our experience is that the hotel will give a discount (which may or may not be the same as the agent's commission), that only meals chosen and eaten have to be paid for, and that a guide is often not needed. There is seldom much difference between a package and the total of our independent costs.

You gain a great advantage in booking as an independent traveller. You don't have to share your dining tables, climb on and off buses in unison, queue to be counted for the morning adventure, or follow the lady waving the red parasol who is talking in an accent that you can't understand. For special tours you have the privacy of your own vehicle, and a personal guide with enough flexibility to make your day very special.

A combination of the scheduled dependent and a non-scheduled independent tour is an acceptable compromise. Arrange the overall travel in detail, with arrival accommodation confirmed in each of the places you intend to visit. Leave local tours and side trips to be booked on arrival. This will give you freedom in timing, to suit the weather and your inclinations. A one-day bus tour around the city with other travellers is endurable and cheap as a rule, and it is easy to organise day by day. It avoids being tied down by prepaid trips on your itinerary that don't seem very interesting now that you are about to go on them. Weather can interrupt; or a local dragon race festival be more appetising than the scheduled visit to the tombs of ancient rulers.

Most veteran Independents will pre-book favoured adventures on short holidays, and use the non-scheduled system for lengthy travel. Experience instils confidence. In our own case, we book the air travel and hotel ourselves by direct fax.

Accumulate all your information, ideas and tentative plans; then seek out a knowledgeable travel agency and let them make the basic reservations for you. *Avoid prepayment of hotels and side trips as much as possible.* The travel agent, in order to safeguard commissions, wants you to prepay everything. Insist that the hotel reservations be made with credit card guarantee, instead of paying in advance. The rub is, if you want to change after you arrive, prepaid vouchers are difficult to get refunds on. The agency's problem is that some hotels are awkward to collect commissions from after you have used their facilities. If the agent insists on payment in advance, then telephone until you find a company that will handle the trip the way you want; or make direct reservations yourself. Most foreign hotels will accept your written or faxed booking, and will be delighted to send a car to meet you at the airport for a nominal charge.

RESEARCH AND PLANNING

As we suggested in Chapter Four, you will want to do intensive research on your intended destinations. Bookshops and the libraries are useful, in particular the reference department. Don't be shy about asking the airlines' major sales arms for specific travel package information. You can use this to guide you, and adopt sections into your own final plans. Consulates or (better) Tourist Departments of foreign nations you plan to see, in or around your (nearest) city, will welcome visits. The advantage is their personnel are often natives of the country or have travelled extensively there. You can develop rapport and receive information with a more human touch than is available from a book.

The secret of Independent Travel is shockingly simple. Except as noted in the previous section, *do not make accommodation or local tour plans until you arrive.* Local travel offices and domestic airlines offer a host of one- to 21-day side trips at economical prices, easily purchased after arrival at any major destination.

Overseas Fly-and-Drive Plans

These usually offer special rates for a vehicle on arrival, and you may find it convenient to start then – especially if the car is delivered to your hotel. The United States, certain Asian countries, Australia and New Zealand are among many places where you will do well with only general advance plans, plus the first hotel – and a car in which to drive yourself at whim.

You can easily start a month in the United States by hiring a vehicle, in advance or on arrival, which you drive away and onto the extensive superhighway network. Inexpensive roadside motels are everywhere, as are meals at the tremendous variety of fast-food and cosy cafes. Disneyland requires no prior reservation, and the side roads off the main highways are well marked. Driving from north to south or coast to coast is simple; you can drop the rented car in almost any major city, and fly back to your departure point.

All of this can be done without pre-vacation bookings. While on the road, telephone ahead from one resting place to another, if you are concerned about an especially busy area. Road maps, travel guides and accommodation listings are readily available. Yes, you may find your first choice of a bed for the night fully booked, but rarely for more than a day or two (tour group or holiday weekend). Alter your plans on impulse, stay longer where you are or find a route round the problem area. Families can rent mini vans or motor-homes, giving a choice between camping grounds, motels or hotels proper – as the mood and pocketbook prompt.

SPECIAL AIR TRAVEL PACKAGES

A Circle Pacific (CP) ticket takes you around the Pacific Rim via any or all of the vast number of sea-cum-airports of the United States, Southeast Asia, Australia, New Zealand, Fiji and Hawaii. The price was US$2,500 per person in 1994, Economy, using selected pairs of airlines. They normally allow six months from gate to gate. You may stop at any destination, in a progressive circle, that one or other airline uses. Four stopovers are included. You pay US$50 more for each extra get-off-and-see port-of-call. Around the World Tickets (AWT) are proportionately more costly; they can involve a maximum of three airlines. The criterion is to proceed always in a single direction, whether easterly or westerly.

We start with CP and AWT information, as these provide the best value for Independent Travellers who have the time and enterprise to travel halfway or completely around the globe, but who prefer a minimum of advance planning. Ask the airlines concerned for the latest information; and then you can book the tickets yourself, or ask your friendly travel agent to do the ticket writing.

Circular route air tickets are the simplest mode of independent travel when you have the time and the wish for such a long journey. Otherwise, round-trip fares to and from an explicit destination are best – in the form of Fly or Fly-and-Drive packages sold by the airlines or their travel-agent subsidiaries.

A CP ticket can include a choice of the following: Los Angeles, San Francisco, Tokyo, Osaka, Beijing, Shanghai, Seoul, Taipei, Hong Kong, Bangkok, Kuala Lumpur, Singapore, Jakarta, Darwin, Perth, Adelaide, Melbourne, Sydney, Brisbane, Townsville, Cairns, Auckland, Christchurch, Nadi and Honolulu. Participating airlines have variants of the circular pattern. They include Qantas, Japan, Singapore, United, Cathay Pacific, British, Northwest, and New Zealand. Most of these also combine for AWT tickets as well.

The plan is flexible enough to allow you to change flight dates during the trip, if space is available. Fares are payable 14 days before departure. An itinerary change en route costs an extra US$100, for the service and the trouble of re-writing. There is no charge for changing a flight date. Frequent-flier mileage may have mounted up, but bear in mind that the 'freebie flight coupons' can be used only for round-trip fares on a single airline. Thus you cannot accumulate mileage towards a free Circle Pacific ticket; but check for overlapping frequent-flier plans. For instance, Qantas mileage accumulates on the American Airlines' 'Advantage' system. Many major airlines have combined their frequent-flier privileges with friendly non-competing lines.

Entry to the CP circuit is available at any of the Pacific Rim airports; AWT from those in Europe as well. Begin by seeking the advice of a convenient participating local airline on either of these marvellous all-encompassing travel systems.

SELF-BOOKING THE AIR TICKET

You are ready. Dates are firm. Destinations and general time limits for each stopover have been agreed. With a calendar, note pad and your information handy, telephone the airline of your first flight. The staff are patient; they work with computers. Take it stop by stop as it is logged on, making your own notes of the flight number, arrival and departure times, and day of the week as well as the date. One major reason for self-booking is that you can make adjustments to dates as you go along, if that is what flight schedules suggest. If you work through an agent, such branching possibilities are likely to be disregarded. On the involved CP and AWT routes, it can be complicated. Do's and don'ts follow:

- "What days do you fly?"
- Where you can, choose the morning departure.
- Use Saturday or Sunday travel dates for uniformity.
- Fully booked? "What is available, plus or minus a day?"
- Book the second best, with the first choice wait-listed/on stand-by.
- "Is this a non-stop flight?"
- "What day or time is there a non-stop?"
- "Is an aircraft or terminal change involved?"
- "How many flying hours between stops?"
- "Is there seat selection? I need leg room."
- "Window seat(s), please."

- "My frequent flier numbers are..."
- "Cancellation and reconfirmation dates?"
- "Ticket purchase deadline?"
- "Please read back what we have agreed."
- "Log number?"
- "Please send a printout by fax or mail."

All right, you are booked, preferably as far in advance as you could plan. Don't worry about changes. You can alter any part of the plan before the ticket purchase deadline. Dates are easily changed en route without charge, subject to seat availability. *Airlines will require you to reconfirm every 30 days until you pay for the ticket.*

Your dates of flying, in the case of extended travel, are easy to change. If you find a better flight – non-stop or with a more convenient departure time – on Tuesday instead of Sunday, take it. Midnight departures are murderous and there is always a chance of confusion over a 12:10 a.m. departure time, as to which the day is. Losing or gaining days over the International Date Line can be confusing when making hotel reservations.

Going from international to domestic terminals – or even from one end of a mammoth airport to another – for aircraft changes, can cause major problems. Your flight may arrive late, you may have to pick up your luggage, or go twice through immigration procedures, meanwhile getting a jitney to the other terminal. The stress level mounts through frustration over finding a luggage cart, and slow queue lines; and you are tired and irritable from the long flight. So leave reasonable time between flights, and ask specifically whether luggage forwarding is handled by the airlines. If it is the same airline it will usually oblige. Boarding a connecting carrier of a different line normally requires you to transfer your luggage.

☛ **Travel Tip**
When reconfirming flights, if you have an airline change *en route*, make sure the initial airline also reconfirms your connecting flight. You have to ask them; they won't do it ordinarily. Connecting flights are often domestic or feeder airlines not hooked up to major computer programs and with no way of knowing of your arrival.

Actually buying the ticket is easy. Your credit card number is sufficient, whether for a telephone purchase or a visit to the nearest sales office. Local travel agents will be delighted to write the ticket for you; they get a commission even though they do no other work. All they need is the log number (see 'Do's and don'ts' above). Be sure to use an agency which writes the ticket on the premises, and verify all the dates and flight numbers with your own information before you leave the office. A lively or aggressive agent will try to sell you additional services. If they book your hotel, you will have to prepay (see below). Let the buyer beware.

Enrol in frequent-flier clubs when you book your air ticket. Sometimes there is a small fee involved, more often it is free. Even though you may never acquire sufficient credits to get a freebie, there are usually some accommodation and car rental discount privileges.

SELF-BOOKING THE HOTEL
Hotels and resorts love to get direct bookings. They save 15–20% on agency commissions. Fax, telephone and address numbers are easily available for major destinations. Give them the date, arrival time, flight information and credit card number with expiry date. Confirmation commits you to a minimum of one night, though this may be cancelled 48 hours before arrival. Take care about the early morning arrival, which may not be on the day you expect. If 12:10 a.m. Thursday is the arrival time, they will have to hold the room for you on Wednesday night.

Unless you have stayed there before, room styles and location descriptions will mean little to you. 'Deluxe' probably means ordinary; 'Superior', the next level; then the luxury suites. Request Superior, with the bed style you prefer and the best rate available. For example: "Superior, king size, mid-level, non-smoking floor, and a business rate would be much appreciated." The business or commercial rate is a discount offered by most hotels. If you are not in business, create one like 'Fisher Travel Partners'. Many hotels will give you an upgrade or a breakfast coupon instead of a discount, if that is their policy. Whatever advantages you can get are welcome. Don't be shy; you won't embarrass the Reservations Manager.

☛ Travel Tip

Ask the name of the person you are talking to. You will refer to this name and its owner's position when you next speak or write to the hotel. Ask them to spell it for you, to make sure you have it right, if you confirm by telephone. On arrival (if not earlier), obtain the names of the General Manager and the Reservations Manager, and include them in your file for the next visit.

Reservations or other requests made to the hotel direct usually put you on a VIP list for extra courtesies on arrival. A personal thank-you letter to the Manager and Staff on leaving is more welcome than filling in the good service form in your room. With modern computer systems, most hotels keep a record of your visit, room style, special services required and your credit card number. When making a reservation for a later visit, always advise them you have been there before.

Many hotel chains have individual club membership systems identifying you as a frequent user. If there is no charge, go ahead and fill out the application. The advantages seem superfluous at first glance, but the major plus is recognition. With a membership card you get reservation preference, often an upgrade and sometimes an extra bowl of fruit and champagne in the room.

Using international reservation numbers is not the same as making a direct reservation. The local international 800 or 008 number connects you with a reservation system operated by the central headquarters of the chain. The hotel actually pays a commission to that exchange, as it does to a travel agent, though with a modified percentage. Contact the hotel direct by phone, fax or letter in order to negotiate a better price.

Most hotel systems – like Shangri-La, Sheraton or Hilton – are hotel management companies. The hotel may be owned by the government, by a private operator or by a consortium hiring the services of the international chain. This gives the owner professional expertise for building and operating the unit, and access to the reservation computer program.

To summarise: treat the system as a fun game. Negotiate prices with a sense of humour and patience. Whatever you save is money in your pocket, allowing you pleasure in another facet of the trip. Make friends wherever you are so that when you return, you are known as a repeat guest. In most instances it will make you feel more comfortable; it might add some unexpected perks; and it could save you some currency.

Independence in travelling is the fifth freedom.

Chapter Six

TRAVEL GUIDES AND HOLIDAY READING

Generally books in a distinctive travel guide series such as *Insight, Lonely Planet, Fielding, Birnbaum,* or *Trav'bug* have a limited shelf-life of one to two years. Check the publication dates before buying. Even those updated and issued every year are about two years old on publication. Basic history and maps do not vary much (except in Russia and some of its neighbours). But accommodation and other facilities are variable as to their service, in real terms and in competition between each other. In aggressive resort areas, new hotels and restaurants continually change anyone's selection of the best places. Old favourites may regress as they age, and be supplanted by newer ones with better facilities and service.

Times Editions' *Culture Shock!* series has a longer shelf-life, since cultures change slowly.

SELECTING A GUIDE BOOK

Guide books have their own market aim. For instance *Lonely Planet* is immensely detailed, published largely for the independent back-packer. These books say much about history, travel systems, accommodation (basic and upward) and street by street detail, but little about fun. *Insight Guide* is much lighter, relegating detail to the end, but well endowed with colour photography. The *Trav'bug* series by Suntree Press is relatively new, and as light and fun-directed as its name implies.

Before purchasing, compare treatments of a single feature. If you are a history buff, you may need more than guides offer. But a casual traveller would find overmuch detail boring, useless and too heavy to carry. Tourist-hungry countries battle each other for cash-flow with new hotels and tour packages. China, in the late seventies, was limited to a handful of historic sites and austere accommodation. Now, there is a broad sweep of hundreds of destinations with comfortable hotels and transport.

Guide books are useful at the start. Some history, culture and map-geography will show where your trail might lead. Arts and crafts are of great interest to the shopoholic. Side trips from major centres are included in the better guides.

A travel guide's function is twofold. For the package-tourist it provides overall information in advance, preparing visitors for the character of the country they hope to enjoy. For Independent Travellers, reading is indispensable. Without it they would not discover, still less be able to select from, all that the world has to offer.

ON-THE-SPOT PUBLICATIONS

Of more immediate use are local books or booklets, bought on arrival. But check the publication dates for the most recent.

STUDY TIME

Many of the guides you might buy are in 800 or more pages of smallish print. One method of studying them is to scan the chapter headings, with an eye on the overall map. Pick out sections to read which deal with the area you might be heading for. There may be a time later for the history and lore. Do not try to read a solid guide as if it were a novel. Like an encyclopaedia, it tells more than any one person could want to know about whichever small corner you will be finding your way about.

You could buy two guides covering the same destination: one with the voluminous detail and the other in a lighter mode, impressive more for its photographs than its larger print. Assuming the cost of your adventure is about US$5,000 for a month's trip, then US$100 for background and foreground material is a very small percentage to invest in print.

Read the fine detail of the area in the guide you have selected. It will often point to you a small, exclusive district or feature not found in the regular tour packages. Travel writers feed their egos with happy finds, off the tourist track. They must whisper the secret somewhere in their pages; and other adventurous souls benefit. Our own scoreboard records eight appearances as first-ever guests. The variety is amusing: the Maharajah's newly-opened tourist rooms in the Shiv Niwas Palace at Udaipur in Rajasthan; Qamea Beach Club off Taveuni, Fiji Islands; and the Pantai Primula new project at Besut, north of Kuala Terengganu on the east coast of West Malaysia – to start with.

Guide books are a help to inexperienced travellers, if used intelligently. Read through and mark the pages you will return to. Use a highlighter to emphasise particular items or paragraphs. Before you set out, do the unthinkable: cut useful pages out and leave the heavy tome at home. (Or, if you are fastidious, duplicate the detail you want to take with you.) Guide books are dated, and of little use a year or two later. Think of your edition as you might of a monthly magazine.

SPEAKING THE LOCAL LANGUAGE

The English language is used throughout the world. Nevertheless, if you plan to spend more than a few days in a country, extract the conversation pages of your guide book or buy a Berlitz-style compact dictionary. Learning how to say hello, thank you, goodbye, plus a few food words, will make your visit more pleasant. The effort will be appreciated by your hosts.

Driving in rural areas may cause some consternation if you have a breakdown or an accident, or if you cannot understand a direction sign. A conversation dictionary can be life-saving then. The third and fourth visits to a country call for some involvement in the culture and the social life. Now it will pay to have more than a smattering of the language and more than a tourist's familiarity with streets, customs and manners.

Once you have become enmeshed you may begin (so long as your interest remains after the novelty has gone) to think in terms of a second home – or even, if the host country permits, permanent settlement.

LITERATURE

There are various levels of book reader. You can pass the time by reading Ludlum's or Clancy's latest spine-tingler. Or you may have been drawn by their fiction to visit the settings of Kipling, Conrad, Hemingway, Maugham or Greene. If so, you are more likely to re-read the books on location, than to pass the time. Hotels now have both semi-advertising and regional history books in their rooms. Newspapers and magazines may provide local colour as well as world events. New novels with (for example) Hong Kong as a background have extra resonance if read while you are in the hyper-city. Bookshops in tourist areas always have a section devoted to local literature.

The point is: read more than 'What's doing in the big city today' while you are in the big city. Historical novels written with local characters are popular. Big coffee-table picture books are too expensive and bulky. Look for paperbacks and Penguin reprints. Prices are modest, but a book you will want to keep is worth half a dozen others.

Literature is the key to a door into greater enjoyment of your travel

Chapter Seven

DESTINATIONS – INTRIGUING, AND ANCESTRAL

TRILL.

There are many ways to choose a travel destination. The easiest is to follow the weekly travel sections of your local newspaper, read the weekend ads and let a target pop out at you. Or perhaps your church group sends a flyer about a specially organised trip to the Falkland Islands; or the local Jockey Club proposes a gourmet tour of France. With this kind of lucky chance you will enjoy a nice trip with friends or family.

Dedicated, innovative, adventurous travellers, eager to see places that have captured their imagination, will do it differently. You may have an overriding urge to photograph every temple and palace; or you may need to climb the highest mountains or sail the longest rivers.

Japan intrigues many travellers. There are strange stories of rituals – and of mixed bathing in hot tubs. Fierce tales, like *Shogun*, relate the frightening experiences of early visitors to the shores of Nippon. Lingering disquiet from the War can inhibit visits to Hiroshima and Nagasaki. Don't let these things deter you; Japan has much to offer the traveller who is free from time restrictions.

China, similarly, remains the tempting culture shock it was to Marco Polo. It is a vast country with so much history that it affects all of us in one way or another. A dozen three- to six-week tours of Old Cathay would barely cover the major scenic and historic wonders.

China and Japan are easily travelled in Independent status, or via one of a host of complex extensive tour packages. Even esoteric countries have made it easy to travel in comfort with or without pre-booked plans. Modern hotels are everywhere; domestic travel agents stand ready to assist with local tours and English-speaking staff. Fears, tremors and trepidations notwithstanding, the adventure is ready for you.

SELECTION

It's a game, and many chapters of this book refer to fun of the sport. Travel is a world board of Monopoly. Roll the dice to decide which part of the globe you will land on first, then second, and so on. Put a good map of the world up on the wall near the breakfast table and contemplate the choices every morning.

The important thing is to obtain as much information as you can about the intended destination. If you plan to travel year after year, start files on the places that intrigue you. Travel is one of the foremost retail industries of our modern world. With few exceptions, distant lands beckon you with open arms, and their districts vie for your business. Write for information, assiduously snip travel articles from newspapers and periodicals, and subscribe to one of the monthly travel magazines. Hotel chains with their links around the world will be delighted to put you on their mailing lists.

THE CONTINENTS
First things first. You have purchased a good traveller's world map such as Bartholomew's, and there it is on the wall. Study the land masses: the Americas, Europe, Africa, Asia – which includes the archipelago of Indonesia with its 17,000 islands – other islands from Australia down to dots like Fiji, Guam, Vanuatu, Samoa, Tahiti and Hawaii.

Start by putting bright-coloured pins in the map at places that intrigue you. Did you see an enticing travel documentary on the television? Put a pin in that area. Or read the Sunday paper with feature articles on the near-fantasy island of Mauritius? Find it on the map and put a pin there. Unless you are a geographer, most of these temptations are merely place-names. The map and pin process connects the names in your vision to their positions on the globe. It becomes clear that when you are in southern India, Sri Lanka and the Maldives aren't too far away. Nepal, Bhutan and Tibet suddenly appear out of nowhere as each others' neighbours – well, almost, because there is no easy highway between them.

The massive island of Australia sits in its own pool of local-name seas between the Indian and Pacific Oceans. New Zealand, looking like separated jigsaw puzzle pieces, becomes part of a path across the Pacific on a line of pins from Sydney to Fiji, Hawaii and Los Angeles. Another line humps over from Los Angeles to Tokyo, curls down through Beijing to Hong Kong, and on to Singapore before it reaches the southern hemisphere with Jakarta and Darwin.

The Circle Pacific air ticket described in Chapter Five makes a sensible pattern as the air route covering the rim destinations of the Pacific Ocean.

FANTASY

According to a fantasy of fiction, an Englishman went 'Around the World in Eighty Days'. Not a bad programme at all, if you keep to it in today's transport. The advantage you have over Phineas Fogg is that you can stay for weeks on each continent during your 80-day odyssey, and enjoy in comfort the distractions of movies and meals while flying on to each new one.

Now, that fantasy can become real. After looking at the world map day after day, you see that no point on the globe is beyond your reach. As each area becomes more familiar, the TV documentaries and Sunday paper travel sections make more sense to you. Clip the latter and save articles in your growing file, first by continent and then by country. As tourist bureaux begin to answer your enquiries, pamphlets and brochures flow in and add to the files. Your bookshelf begins to fill with publications. Assemble travel stories and novels that relate to these areas, near the files, to re-read when you have time. They will maintain the enthusiasm.

The newest sales tool is the video tape. Many advertisers will send a free tape of an area on request. Video rental libraries are starting sections on geography, and publications such as *National Geographic* offer tapes for sale on projects they have published.

You are now changing the fantasy to possibility. Soon the possibility metamorphoses into reality, and the destination daydreams become real plans. Before you know it, the time has come. You have bought your tickets, packed your bags, boarded the aeroplane and flown across the seas. You are about to arrive in what once was the never-never-land of your imagination.

VISITING THE ANCESTORS

Alex Haley, author of the famous novel (and hence of the film) *Roots*, traced his origins with great difficulty and trepidation. They became another written history of the slave trade in North America. No less importantly, the story revealed to the inhabitants of present-day Africa their own roots. Few of us are not tied to a former nationality, race or mix of races.

Fed by old photographs, there is a curiosity in many people to follow that tie back to the land of their ancestors. Immigrant families know where the grandparents once lived. The urge to travel often combines with the instinct to go back to the original soil and to seek out relatives – some heard of, some not.

Welcome?

Do not rely on your welcome in the land of your forefathers. Government attitudes in ancestral nations vary. Foreign-born members of the Chinese race are known in the PRC as Overseas Chinese. A special branch (China Travel Service or CTS) of the travel company, Luxingshe, books them separately from other foreigners (handled by China International Travel Service or CITS). Different hotels and coaches keep local and overseas Chinese from being 'contaminated' by other travellers. This will be explained to you in detail when you apply to any of the Luxingshe International Travel offices.

(We know of a non-Chinese couple who were advised by Chinese friends in Macau to try the CTS office as its tour to Hainan was at half the CITS price. Everything else was the same except that only Cantonese was spoken by the tour party. Our friends enjoyed a week as mascots, cosseted with fragments of Hong Kong English. They recommend Hainan to all who fancy a large tropical island, with huge empty beaches, that is also part of 'Mainland China'. Alas, things may be stricter now.)

Many other countries distinguish between foreign nationals, with and without local family origins. Some authoritarian governments are suspicious or hostile, while others enthusiastically welcome potential 'cash cow' pilgrims. You can find out how the land lies only from 'compatriots' who have recently 'been home'. The written rules may not be the actual state of affairs after you cross the border.

Sometimes the family welcomes you with open arms seeking gifts. In countries under tight government control, there are two special kinds of culture shock: first from officials, and then, perhaps, from the kith and kin. You are seen as Rich Relatives by those who have no freedom of travel or lifestyle. Thus you may be expected to bring a plethora of presents, to spend money entertaining the extended local family at banquets, and to promise monthly stipends thereafter. Unfortunately you, the average person, earn (or used to earn) a modest income – and are probably stretching the budget for the pleasure of meeting them.

No doubt you are rich by comparison of lifestyle, but that does not necessarily provide hundreds of your currency for a banquet. Nor is it always convenient to travel with two or three large cartons of television sets as gifts for expected and unexpected uncles and aunts.

One could write ahead but with no definite dates, to keep the visit uncertain and low key. Or, even less courageously, one can arrive unheralded and decide to move on or not once one has taken a view of the family and its welcome.

The freer the country the more normal the reception of visiting *émigrés* by government and family. The branches of some families will have remained in touch with the tree over the generations, while others have little except a name to trace.

If the trip is largely for the sake of the ancestral visit, you will not need extensive travel plans. Writing ahead to known relatives or to the local tourist information centre should obtain all you need to know. Do not let your travel agent sell you anything besides the transport. This is no time to be saddled with prepaid side trips.

It is necessary, however, to read up your family's history and original geography. If there seems to be no one of your name where there should be, bear in mind that marriages and the hazards of pronunciation may have changed yours. Check back on your forebears long before you go. Remember the stories your mother or grandmother told about your origins. Create a family tree to the best of your knowledge; with luck you will then not be surprised to meet Cousin Wu or Uncle Joseph. If you have a photograph which enables you to guess his name right, he will be delighted. You, of course, will be trading news of the overseas members for what you learn from those who stayed. Indeed you may have been better placed to preserve some of the traditions than they. They may find it harder to picture the land and its ways as they used to be. You, the travellers, may be more, or less, curious about what you do and do not have in common.

Exploring your roots can be an enjoyable and enlightening experience. Take lots of photographs – with you and while there. A small tape recorder is a great help in taking notes and preserving the voices of the current generation, for relatives in either country. Video cameras are better value for both sides than gimmicky polaroids, since replay equipment is in use almost everywhere.

Chapter Eight

MEANS OF TRANSPORT

There is great emphasis today on air travel. We are in a hurry to get there; time limitations, and the major packages offered, point us towards the airport. Air travel is indeed the primary mode, but alternatives should be considered – as adventures in themselves or as useful or pleasant supplements. You are setting out to see the world, but you won't see much from 35,000 feet. Ships, trains, buses, cars, motor boats, canoes, bicycles and feet – all these keep one close to the visible surface of the earth.

BY AIR

The key to air travel is physical comfort. Once you are on board and settled down after take-off, the ride is similar to sitting in an armchair for the next 6 to 12 hours. Which, of course, few people willingly do. Discomfort increases as time passes and the ambience deteriorates. Your clothes become wrinkled, debris accumulates around you, boredom sets in, you are tired of reading and you can't sleep comfortably.

Before boarding, prepare all the articles you might want. Keep handy: reading matter and writing materials, puzzles, a pillow if you use one, your passport (to fill out arrival documents), a headache remedy, and sweets if they help with swallowing or the nerves. It is frustrating to dig out something you need from your luggage, especially when people are waiting to get to their seats. Opening the storage compartment above you in flight is dangerous. If you use a cart for your baggage, detach it before boarding. Take advantage of a toilet in the concourse before you go to the loading bay.

Eat lightly, save the cheese and crackers for a later snack; drink lots of liquid but little, if any, alcohol.

In-flight Exercise
Constant air-travellers have their own routines for limbering up the stiffening muscles. Watch for these rare flying birds. If you see one, get up and copy the performance. (This assumes that you fear discomfort more than the whole process of flying. Otherwise, stay within your seatbelt, as advised in Chapter Three.)

If you do nothing to prevent it, your feet and ankles swell, and your back aches from trying to find a comfortable position (there isn't one). *Conquer Fear of Flying*, a short book written by an Australian pilot, has a good chapter on exercises. The author is indebted to Shanti Gowans, a teacher of yoga, for a series of in-flight toners.

Basically the advice is common sense. Get out of the seat and stretch the arms, do knee bends and torso twists. Meditation, deep breathing, eye-swivelling exercises, and limited isometrics – these are all well-known stress and body relievers. There are pages of detail, none of which will be remembered unless you put them into regular practice for weeks beforehand. Do not despair, though. Merely strolling the aisles does much to ease the strain. And if, nevertheless, you suffer discomfort – well, you will forget it once the plane lands and excitement takes over.

PASSENGER SHIPS

The oceans, seas, rivers and lakes cover much more of the earth's surface than land does. If you can afford it, and you get the chance, consider a voyage on the *QE2* – the liner *Queen Elizabeth the Second.* This, the most majestic ship afloat, crosses the Atlantic between Southampton and New York in a little over four days, usually as part of a longer cruise.

Whichever your ship, instead of being scrunched into a bucket on an aircraft, you will have a cabin of your own, decks on which to amble, walk, jog or run, games to play, fine food and wine, entertainment, and a host of people to serve your every need and whim.

Continent-to-continent passenger ships are becoming rare. Shipping lines or the cruise departments of port authorities are more likely than travel agents to know about them.

CRUISE SHIPS

Luxury cruise ships are floating five-star hotels, in which you both stay, and move – for a few days, a few weeks, or as long as it takes to circle the globe. As you would expect of luxury hotels, they are more expensive than other modes of travel, day for day. However, it is inclusive: you are paying both for your stay and for your passage. You may dine on caviar, foie gras, lobster or quail fondue to your heart's content, and the wine that goes with them is probably included. Other drinks are extra – as are the expected healthy tips. Ports may be explored independently, or you may add organised tours to your accumulating account.

There are levels of market in cruise ships as in other travel modes. You should do your own research, here as elsewhere. Agencies shout the delights of the luxury liners, television commercials depict their romance, and bargain-price ads are common. First, select the time, the area you wish to see, and a level of luxury. These last two sometimes interconnect. Cruising down the Yangtze River is one style, taking a Caribbean or Mediterranean voyage is another. Season is extremely important, as cruises are limited by weather. The same ship will sail the South Seas in January and Norwegian fjords from May to September.

Cost is affected by the luxuriousness and length of travel. Long cruises can be joined and left at intermediate ports. The normal system is to book months in advance on the cruise of your choice, pay the price and enjoy the luxury of the voyage. Air connections are usually included in the quoted price of the package, from and to your home airport. You cannot save money and negotiate prices by booking directly with the company unless, perhaps, you know one of its administrative staff. However, last-minute passages are offered by certain discount operators to fill empty cabins (see pages 73–4).

Take as much luggage as you wish; other than in and out of your car, it will be handled by porters. On the most luxurious liners, dress is formal for dinner, especially if you are invited to dine at the Captain's table on one evening. Other ships require jacket and tie for men and cocktail dresses for women.

☛ Security Caution

Cruise ships are notorious for sophisticated thefts of jewellery and valuables. People become casual, and cabin locks are easy to pick. So use the Purser's lock-up boxes.

Mahjong, poker and bridge games for high stakes with strangers are foolhardy. By all means play the slots and the tables. The *croupiers*, at least, smile when they take your money.

Dining Aboard a Cruise Ship

The normal arrangements are four, eight or twelve people pre-assigned to a table by the *maître d'*. After boarding and before you unpack, go directly to the dining room and identify the head man. If you are travelling as a pair, you might make the following statement after introducing yourself: "We wish to dine in the second seating and will require a deuce for privacy. This is our honeymoon and a romantic corner would be greatly appreciated." The protocol is to accompany this with a US$20 or US$50 bill (depending on the length and luxuriousness of the voyage) folded and visible in the hand. A deuce, in dining room vernacular, is a table for two. Those in the know always dine late, since the first sitting is asked to clear the dining room by a fixed time.

But you may prefer the time and places allotted to you: either because the first session gives more scope for evening activities, or through enjoying the company of like-minded travellers. But, while you will not necessarily choose a table full of your own countrymen, you will want a common language. So you should still find out how you are seated – and if need be, make your wishes known – as soon as you can; but the dollar ritual will not be needed.

On a cruise ship, problems may arise through a combination of close quarters and the engineered social events. The crew assigned to conviviality continually work to get people together and arrange an endless array of entertainment. If you are a single looking for company, or a couple willing to make new friends, the programmes should suit you. Sign up for almost everything. Two people on a special anniversary voyage as a romantic interlude will take a different view, though.

☞ Personal Experience
My wife and I booked a cruise in the Caribbean many years ago. We succeeded in dining alone every night except when

invited to the Captain's table. We won a bottle of champagne and a set of eight gold decorated bar glasses for first place in a ballroom dancing contest, with our tribute to Fred Astaire and Ginger Rogers. A friendly chef arranged to share his personal loot of beluga caviar, obtained in barter with a Russian cruise ship tied up next to us in Jamaica. He had to serve with the can concealed under some foliage so that people at the next table would not ask for the same – a rare experience of the furtive habits of the Rich and Famous. Yes, we exchanged a padded handshake on our departure, knowing that we had enjoyed our money's worth.

The Growing Cruise Industry

Increasingly, there are non-luxury cruise ships and ships with sub-luxury classes of accommodation. As some holiday towns are almost taken over at certain times by free-spending workers of this or that nation, so you on a cruise ship may be surrounded by one language and several of its speakers' lifestyles. The expanding industry could not survive on travellers who can afford gracious sailing. It seeks to serve the middle and enterprising other classes, with short cruises (even weekend 'Cruises to Nowhere') while they are still working – and with longer ones later.

Reduced rates are offered by cruise lines surreptitiously through discount vendors. This is their way of filling cabins shortly before sailing, just as airlines fill seats. For you, it provides a last-minute chance to take advantage of a holiday which you would in any case find attractive. Book provisionally, with an agency, one or more cruises during a period when you expect to be free. Make it clear that you will confirm a booking only on being offered a late bargain. The agent will telephone two or three days before a sailing date, offering (say) a second-deck cabin at 40% discount on the good ship *Whatever*, sailing from Hong Kong to Shanghai, Qingdao, Yokohama, Taipei and back to Hong Kong. You answer 'yes' or 'no' on the spot, before the vendor tries the next client on his list. The return air ticket to Hong Kong is also discounted, as part of the package.

Watch for advertisements of these specials in travel journals and weekend newspaper travel sections. If it is not a well-known agency you could verify its credibility with a travel organisation or society, but it is perfectly in order to call a cruise line direct to verify the offer of the agency. But sometimes you might be lucky enough to land a late-offered cruise without going through the nerve-stretching procedure described in the previous paragraph.

FREIGHTERS

A little-known and (so far) seldom used mode of sea travel is the limited passenger accommodation on several of the world's sea-freight lines. Shipping companies have found it profitable to sell cabin space on semi-scheduled and non-scheduled routes. Passengers may book 10-day round trips or 100- to 150-day round-the-world voyages; or go halfway and fly back (or vice versa); or ingeniously take a long sea passage, instead of a flight, before or after a foreign posting. This last may be hampered by ships' tendency to circumnavigate eastwards. Prices per diem are reasonable (US$90–130 in 1994) since the rate varies as to time and distance, and includes services on board. Air passages are not included and may be difficult to secure, though the organisation that arranges your booking may undertake to book a matching flight.

Few travel agents know about freighters. If you do not wish to deal direct with shipping companies or through a coordinator (such as the two mentioned below), you might find a local travel agency willing to explore the options on your behalf. The commission would be 10% or less of a large sum of money. You may wish to tempt your own enterprising agent with a copy of these paragraphs...

Newsletters are available, for the most part mimeographed monthly productions by *aficionados* of the system. More formal

information will come from large shipping lines listed in the telephone book and from shipping pages of port-city newspapers. The freight lines will tell you whether they take passengers and where to find details. We offer two addresses: Freighter World Cruises of 180 Lake Street, Suite 335, Pasadena, CA 91101, USA, tel: (818) 449 3106, fax: 449 9537; and The Strand Cruise and Travel Centre, Charing Cross Shopping Concourse, London WC2N 4HZ, UK, tel: 836 6363, fax: 497 0078. Strand deals on behalf of 35 shipping companies which between them take from 2 to 12 passengers on 60 set voyages between Europe, Africa, the Middle and Far East, Australia, New Zealand, the Pacific islands, South and North America, Russia, the Baltic and Iceland.

Freighters provide the ultimate in Independent Travel. You book to sail on a particular ship, from Sydney, say, in the first week of May. The ship will call at New Zealand ports before heading across the Pacific for the Panama Canal. If there is a choice, ask for the largest cabin on the main deck forward, with bow-facing porthole. You pay an advance and you take your chance.

All being well, the shipping line calls you and advises that you should board at 6:00 p.m. on the 3rd of May at Pier #6. The first port of call will be Auckland. Eventually a smiling Captain and First Officer welcome you aboard; you are shown to a roomy cabin and told that dinner will be served in the Officers' Mess as soon as the ship has cleared the harbour. Two couples of different nationalities are already on board; you gather with them on deck below the bridge to watch the departure. One or two months later, you will have visited ports in a dozen countries, read two dozen books, piled up ten rolls of exposed film, written all your letters, and become so completely rested that you are looking ahead for your next adventure. Also you will be watching the intricacies, as the ship enters your last harbour, with something like a seaman's eye.

All the shipping companies impose an upper age limit: some as high as 79 or 80. All require doctors' certificates for passengers over 65, and special insurance cover. The ship provides food and comfort, but you make your own entertainment. Time in port is seldom more than a day; a passenger might set foot in three Australian cities but, unless one is the port of embarkation or disembarkation, will scarcely have seen the country.

Mail is sent and received at each port of call. Passengers may use fax at sea. There are no luggage restrictions; indeed your trunks may go on to your destination, if you complete your journey by air. My publishers are pleased to note three standard voyages which will land passengers in Singapore, but have found none that will take them away.

We hope this section of the book will produce new 'Deluxe Economy ' seafarers. And we hope more shipping companies will make that possible by putting spare cabins to good use.

RIVER CRUISES

River cruises are less expensive, since they entail shorter voyages. They are booked as parts of longer itineraries, or are joined as side trips by Independent Travellers as opportunities occur. In China for instance, a Yangtze River voyage takes you through the famous Three Gorges, upriver for five to seven days or down-river for three or four. Some of these cruise ships are operated by the Chinese government, others by joint venture companies. Tickets include food, guides, shore trips, and either a return to the point of embarkation by other means or the next stage of an onward journey.

Adventurous travellers may book on the standard people's passenger and freight ferries for only the price of conveyance. These are much cheaper, and permit breaks of journey for a few hours or days at places of interest. You may start at Chongqing, go ashore at Wuhan, Lushan or Nanjing, stay a few days at each port and continue as far as Shanghai after a fortnight.

One fascinating way to see the northwestern coastal waters of North America is to take the daily car-passenger ferry out of Seattle and sail north for some 750 miles along the coast of Canada. This is more ambitious than a river cruise. Having started amidst islands in the sounds and inlets of Washington State, you may choose to finish in Anchorage, Alaska, via the 150-mile Cook Inlet – overlooked by the Aleutian Range. Luxury cruise ships ply this route less adventurously, but the do-it-yourself traveller may prefer mingling with the back-packers and Alaskan residents in stop-and-stay-awhile ports.

Major rivers offer lengthy water journeys: the Mississippi in the United States, the Murray in Australia, the Mekong between Laos and Myanmar and then between Laos and Thailand and through Cambodia and Vietnam, the Nile in Egypt and the Amazon in South America. You may choose between tourist comfort and the reality of Mekong rice barges.

Slow Long Boats

Canal barges in England and France give homely comfort rather than chrome luxury, soothing rather than dramatic scenery, and all the independence of driving a car. The holiday industry and canal enthusiasts have restored pre-lorry, pre-railway trade routes and the pubs, inns and *auberges* which served them. In some countries 'houseboat' means much the same as 'canal barge'; in others a houseboat is static – a floating residence or, in Kashmir, a floating hotel-chalet. Information on inland waterway travel is easily found in the better travel guides covering the area of interest.

One-Day River Boat Trips

Day trips afloat abound in all countries with water systems. You will uncover many in the guide books and other literature acquired in your research. Some, more esoteric, are discovered when you get there. The Li Chiang River near Guilin in China is historically famous. Joining an armada of 50 other crowded tourist boats is an experience sought by some but shunned by others. Queensland offers an Australian river trip in the Daintree rain forest where you can commune, at a distance, with monstrous crocodiles. The Murray River further south, like the Mississippi, has nostalgic paddle steamers offering one-day or longer trips.

Port cities always offer scenic boat tours of the harbour and adjacent shore line. Auckland, New York, Sydney, San Francisco, Singapore and Hong Kong provide excellent views of the city from the sea. They cost little, often taking only an hour, and give good value.

COASTAL STEAMERS

Coastal steamers are deep-water ships plying coastal routes, as craft have for hundreds of years. They carry passengers and freight cheaply, and are usually ignored by travel agents and package tours. We think highly of this mode of travel and book passages whenever conveniently available. Despite their modest prices, most ships have cabin accommodation, reasonable food (but you may bring your own), and a characteristic ambience. Those stopping at several ports offer a few hours or a day ashore to explore. *Keep within hearing distance of the ship's whistle or siren.*

Travel is leisurely; fellow passengers, predominantly natives of the country, are nearly always friendly. Crew members are helpful to foreign passengers. In most cases you can visit the bridge or engine room on request, listen to the constant jargon on the communication radio, and enjoy moonlit nights at sea.

Examples are: Shanghai to Hong Kong or Shanghai to Qingdao; Seattle to ports of Alaska; Java to Ujung Pandang in Sulawesi to Ambon in the Moluccas and Denpasar in Bali, all in the Indonesian archipelago. Japan offers short voyages between the three major islands: Yokohama to Hokkaido and Kobe to Beppu are unique and enjoyable short voyages in the Sea of Japan.

Booking a coastal steamer follows the train-ticket procedure, with published timetables (see the next page). Most hotels and local travel agencies keep tabs on this mode of travel.

We have had poor food from time to time (in China) but never an uninteresting voyage. Every coastal trip we have taken has been happily memorable. Coastal steamers are the least expensive, while often the least luxurious, mode of 'Economy Deluxe' travel. Always enquire about likely weather and sea conditions. A rough sea trip is no fun.

BY TRAIN

As described by the novelist and travel writer, Paul Theroux, the railway train is a monster, a wonderful experience, a veritable buffet of adventure in many lands. Super-fast bullet trains now exceed 125 mph and go from city centre to city centre in times that equal flight travel. Major stations are in city or town centres, with easy access; boarding takes a minimum amount of time; and trains are even safer than aircraft.

Rail travel is especially suited to the Independent Traveller, as it entails little advance planning – though you would undoubtedly need to organise a journey on the Trans-Siberian Railway or the Orient Express, whether from London to Venice or from Bangkok to Singapore.

A day's notice or two will secure a Pullman compartment (see next page) on an all-day express train. Avoid 'milk runs': trains that start early and stop at every small station become tedious. It is usually possible to reserve seats for journeys of less than 24 hours since extra reservations justify a longer train. For overnight journeys, book sleeping berths unless you won't mind most of the disadvantages of a very long flight.

Cross-country trips are notable successes in some countries. Europe is famous for good train equipment, which supports a traditional means of travel. Eurorail passes are available for modest prices, allowing unlimited travel within a fixed period. South Africa has its Blue Train from Johannesburg to Cape Town. Canada provides a magnificent transcontinental scenic route from Victoria to Montreal. In the United States, Amtrak is improving the cross-country routes; and Mexico has quite interesting trips from the US border southwards. Australia, with vast distances to cross, has modern equipment and good prices, offering an excellent change from hurried flight schedules.

Worldwide, train travel has the easiest booking arrangements. You consult the timetable, buy a ticket at the station, find the right platform, board the train and away you go. A city's tourist office will send details on request, which will highlight scenic routes.

On-the-spot information is available from your hotel or from helpful members of the public. For many people railways are a part of their way of life, and often a source of pride. They will offer advice as to the best routes and times, from personal experience. Only floods or snowstorms are likely to disrupt rail traffic.

Longer routes usually have at least two levels of comfort, First Class and Second Class. At the bottom is the bench car, described in China as 'Hard Seat'. Sleeping berths can be bunks stacked three high, non-reserved. First Class sometimes equates with Chair Car or 'Soft Seat'; but seats in many countries' Second Class are not hard, and can be reserved. First Class is good 'Economy Deluxe', with reserved cushioned seats, and refreshments sold en route and at stops. Special compartments – called Pullman after the originator of sleeper travel – give privacy; they are usually sold on a four-occupant basis.

We recommend reserving a whole compartment for any train trip over eight hours. In some systems you book a compartment as a unit. In others, particularly major train travel areas like China and India, you have to buy all four seats to ensure privacy. Watch out for the porter, whose job it is to convert the seats to bunks, where no bed is visible.

Train travel is hypnotising, with the constant methodical chatter of wheels to rails. For a daytime journey it's very pleasant to stretch out, doze and arrive rested. Sleeping on a train at night is a mixed blessing. The clackety-clack is restful, but the train stopping and starting always wakes me up.

Dining Cars

The walk along the swaying train and the distraction of the meal make an interesting interlude. On a luxury train, the food and the service can be more of a pleasure than an adventure. Down the scale, the reverse is likely. Even so, coffee and cake or a couple of beers and some rice add up to a pleasant diversion. On a high-class train, enquire as soon as you board about table reservations; as you would on a cruise ship, ask for the second sitting. You can then dawdle with a bottle of wine over an extended dinner and leisurely coffee.

☛ **Travel Tip**

Where equipment and facilities are old, or there are doubts about hygiene, think twice about taking a 24-hour journey. Toilets may be even less comfortable than those in aircraft. And it will be better to buy packaged food and fruit at the train stops, and to carry your own swag-bag with snacks.

As against this advice, we should record the testimony of two non-spartan families who travelled by rail at different times in the 1980s from the Pacific Coast to Moscow. They experienced much friendliness and little hardship.

BY COACH OR BUS

'And leave the driving to us' is the famous advertising slogan of the Greyhound Line in the United States. Travelling by bus is a mixed bag of adventure, leisure and comfort; on the other side of the coin it can be miserably confining and boring. There are few general rules to be applied other than the constant: *Do your research, ask the right questions.*

Package Tours by Coach

Generally for seven to 21 days, package tours use modern air-conditioned vehicles, with experienced drivers and a guide. Schedules and scenic routes are well planned, through repetition, and you know approximately what you are in for before you start.

If you can, fly early to the departure destination and spend a couple of days in the city to orient yourself; then join the tour as scheduled. Such a tour is an excellent way to view the land, in a country you haven't visited before. It introduces you to areas that may turn out to be so interesting that you will return the following year, to stay longer in a good spot.

Many tours can be booked on arrival – during your two-day reconnaissance, as it were – allowing your selection to be influenced by weather and a wider range of options. In the high season expect weekly or twice-weekly departures on the popular longer trips.

Advantages of Coach Tours

You know where you must be and when, and where you will be taken. Your luggage will be handled efficiently; hotels and most meals will be of predictable standards, though in unpredictable surroundings; you will have with you a group of like-interest travel companions; and everything that needs to be is pre-booked. The best of local sights are enjoyed without preamble or the business of selecting them.

Since the coach will always pick you up, you lose no time – as you do getting to and waiting at airports. There is ample space to stow your hand-luggage and shopping trophies. A general air of conviviality is felt after the first few hours, when names and home towns are exchanged.

Disadvantages of Coach Tours

The snags include petty annoyances over which seat is best; other passengers who ignore the timetable, constantly holding up the bus; and sometimes a guide who hogs the microphone or deafens with his foreground music.

Shopping stops are too few or too short for you and too many and too long for someone else. Lunch and other pit stops at wayside cafes may range from adequate to various degrees of miserable.

Some older tourists look tired as they leave their coach at the end of the day, exasperated perhaps with queuing up for room keys and restaurant tables; they are rarely seen to smile or laugh. Other members gather in cliques to gossip about the day's events and the morrow's prospects – complaining or enthusing. A whole day of activity is tiring and boring, or exhilarating and memorable, usually as you choose to make it.

If the trip is long and becomes unbearable, cut your losses, rent a car and continue the adventure individually. If you plead health problems, you may be able to get a partial refund.

Crosscountry Public Buses

This is a different story. To see the country and leave the driving to the professionals is a fine way to enjoy exploration, free of pre-booked itinerary – especially if you are adventurous and impulsive. As with train travel, pass tickets may allow you to stop for a day or more and catch an onward bus. As an alternative to a hotel or motel, Bed-and-Breakfast rooms are the vogue in many places, aiming for a family-style house-guest stay. (A 'guest house' is closer to the hotel concept.) Unplanned, a visit to a quaint village or small town is a rare treasure, since the unknown can be more exciting than the expected. The bus depot normally has a public information service to help arrange accommodation.

Japan's standard fixed-route buses are uniformly excellent. Schedules are minute-precise and drivers always stop at scenic views for picture taking. Other passengers are friendly, despite the language barrier. Every lunch place we encountered in Japan was delightful, with a beautiful view and a full meal menu or the alternative of a superior snack. Toilets and washrooms were refreshingly clean.

In some countries, however, I would never buy a ticket for a bus I hadn't seen. Brochures hyped with grandiose pictures of fine equipment, gorgeous scenery and quiet highways may conceal reality: buses which have seen better days, scenery turned urban, crowded and overhung by smog. The bus could fill with chickens, pigs and squalling children. Arrange a chauffeured vehicle or drive yourself, unless the bus is visibly modern and the itinerary specified.

Transport depots in some larger cities are not particularly inviting for the sophisticated traveller, being generally in older, seedier parts of the metropolis. You are wise to watch your purse and valuables while waiting, and be well placed in the queue – for a seat towards the front. Once on the road, the ambience is more pleasant. If in doubt, go to the depot before you buy the ticket and see the general condition of the vehicles. An hour spent in investigation could save you days of discomfort.

Besides North America and Japan, Malaysia and most European countries have good long-distance bus systems. One can take local journeys, anywhere, without thorough investigation, and enjoy the flavour of the country as well as its countryside. In many less developed countries a taxi from town to town is invitingly cheap, if you agree on the fare before you start.

☛ **Travel Tip**
Combine a train and bus trip. For instance, in the US, take the Amtrak from Los Angeles to Chicago, Denver or New Orleans. Then join the Greyhound and explore to the north, the east or the south; and then decide whether to go back by train or bus.

Mini Vans
Mini vans are quite common in Southeast Asia and resort areas elsewhere. They suit uneven road surfaces. With six to eight people in tighter but more informal seating, a sociable spirit quickly develops. This spirit normally includes the driver, who is likely to be affable and informative. It is easier to divert a van than a coach after a road accident or trouble from floods. Enquire at tourist information centres on arrival: by scouting around you may find someone who has recently taken the trip that interests you. First-hand information is always the best way to find out about comfort on such excursions.

Adventurous safari trips explore rain forests, the outback and other happily uncivilised areas with six- to eight-passenger four-wheel drive land cruisers. There are basic hostels, or tent camps are set up at night. This is 'Deluxe Back-packing': you can explore remote areas in some degree of catered comfort.

BY HIRE CAR
Hertz, Avis, Budget and other international names are as famil-

iar as Kodak and Coca Cola in most of the travel world today. Sedans/saloons, mini vans, 4WD rugged vehicles, campers with built-in facilities, topless/convertibles, windowless mokes, motor and pedal cycles, etc. are available for hire. With the proper self-confidence, and a credit card to back up your verve and enthusiasm, rent a vehicle and drive it yourself. International road markings are uniform on major highways; information books are provided for the local 'sign language'. Hire at one end of a country and drop the car off at the other end.

Cruising down a highway or byway in a foreign land with your favourite travelling companion, when it suits you, is the acme of Independent Travel. It is pure freedom to drive through the spring or autumn countryside of Italy, Portugal or Spain, and stop at an ancient hillside walled village. Brush aside the beaded entrance of a roadside cafe, order the house wine, cheese, fruit and a crusty loaf. Sign language and a few words of courtesy will leave both sides smiling. You will remember the sun, the smiles and the taste of the wine and cheese for many years.

FLY AND DRIVE

Major international airlines provide fly-and-drive packages. This is a simple arrangement between the carrier and the car rental agency. Fly to your foreign airport and pick up a reserved car to be used for the period specified, which can be from one day to one month. Some of these arrangements include hotel/motel accommodation along a specified tour route. It is a common practice to buy the combination and not use the rooms unless they suit you. This 'throwaway' package is cheaper than buying the air ticket and car rental separately.

Alternatively, major car rental agencies offer longer international packages at reduced rates, if you book before you leave. The nearest office of the agency will provide the information you need and do the booking for you. Coupon tie-ins for car rental and hotels accompany frequent-flier award certificates.

Members of airline clubs are offered special rates for overseas travel. Ask the car rental agency about membership of their frequent-user or commercial clubs. Don't worry about building up enough mileage credits: you may or may not, but at least they will give you a price advantage in booking.

BUY AND DRIVE

A shrewd traveller will arrange to buy the next Mercedes in Germany, tour in it for weeks or months and then ship it home. This cuts out middlemen, some import fees and the cost of hiring a car during the holiday. Caution: investigate all the rules of the game long before you make a commitment.

HIRE CAR WITH DRIVER

Many countries have strict regulations about foreign drivers. They require an international driver's licence and insurance bonds. In some places, the only foreigners allowed to drive are diplomatic and business residents. An example is China where you book a car and driver, for a short or a long period, through the China International Travel Service.

The good side of this is the safety and pleasure of sightseeing free from the distraction of driving. A day's tour of the city and surrounding countryside is better enjoyed with a driver. Even a week or two on the road with a driver-guide is usually very pleasant, given a congenial driver. Costs are often less than you imagined, as the driver's bed and board are complimentary, in most areas, recognising that he has brought you as paying guests to the domain. Language is seldom a problem as the hire company aims to provide an English-speaking driver. Once in China, and once in Japan, our driver spoke no English. With maps, conversation/translation guides and general goodwill we had no problems of significance. In fact it was pleasant to teach each other bits of our languages.

Furthermore, there would be the strain of driving yourself,

perhaps not on your usual side of the road, through metropolitan traffic of frightening density. Would you really like to drive your own car on the Champs Elysées in Paris, knowing what pictures have shown you of that tooting tangle?

We avoid driving in big cities like London, New York, Paris, Bangkok, Manila or Jakarta. Strangers should be wary of the roads of Sri Lanka, India and Nepal, for example. But, away from huge cities, you should enjoy consistently good roads and well marked motorways in most European countries, Malaysia, North America, Australia and elsewhere.

Advantages of Car Hire

It is nice to have a car handy in a resort area for local travel. The convenience of getting around and the pleasure of wheels immediately available enlarge the scope of the area immensely. You can try to resolve the matter with a cash equation: "How many days will we be using the vehicle, as against bus adventures and taxi fares?" But this may make you miss the real advantage: if you have a car, you will go out more and will therefore see more countryside, eat at more restaurants and have the largely paid-in-advance freedom to go and come on impulse.

TREKKING: THE A, B AND C SPORT

The trick in trekking (or hiking, or walking) is to know thyself and thy limitations. The Chinese call walking the #11 taxi or bus, referring to the two legs. The sport of using one's built-in locomotion is vast, the participants grading themselves into the A, B or C level depending on their physical fitness and expertise.

A's are the past-masters and for the most part will not be reading this text, having their own journals. Their field includes crossing mountain ranges and wildernesses. Cliff scalers and mountain climbers are extreme examples of this group.

B's are very good, primarily using the sport for travel enjoyment; they can endure a three- to five-day crosscountry adventure with little stress. They keep up their physical condition year by year, attuned to many-mile hikes as weekly exercise. Age is rarely a factor, as you can see in Switzerland where octogenarians are commonly found on the longest trails. The B trekkers will seek out walking-tour vacations oriented to their ambitions. They sometimes associate with the A's on lesser mountains for training or to upgrade their ability.

C's include the rest of us. Novices, people who like to walk their five miles a day or swim a few lengths in the pool each morning. If in generally good physical condition most of us, regardless of age, can enjoy organised jungle treks for example. We may lag behind now and then, stopping to rest more often than some, but will wind up at the starting place. Don't try this sort of thing on the first day of your vacation; rest up and take a hike along the beach to get in breathing shape. If you habitually swim, run or row, that will be fine for your general fitness; but you will also need some walking practice. The muscles are not the same.

Your enjoyment is considerably reduced if you do not have physical comfort. Find out exactly the best kind of shoes and clothing to wear. Carry as little as you can, in a light back-pack. Leave your arms free in case you have to grab a branch or tree root for support. If you start panting, as you climb the first tier of 50 steps, stop and settle the heartbeat before continuing. I relate the following experience as the best advice possible for occasional trekkers.

☛ Personal Experience

We were enjoying a Greek tour, booked on a whim one year with a Swiss travel agent. We had no idea what the itinerary was. The ship was a freighter turned cruise ship, our group mixed German and Swiss. We anchored off an island in the morning. The party went ashore to trek across the island and meet the ship in the afternoon on the other side. A Swiss doctor and family befriended us, having long experience of legging it in their native land. Dr Franz noticed my flushed, panting condition (at the age of 50), struggling to keep up with the group ascending a hill. My wife, a perennial walker, had no problems.

"Fritz (he converted my name), walk behind me. We are going to slow the pace – one foot at a time – and not worry about the others." We walked slowly, rarely stopping except when the group halted for *ouzo* at a roadside cafe or a lunch of fresh olives and *feta* cheese. By the end of the day, we were far ahead of the group, my pulse regular; I was breathing normally and felt comfortably tired. What I most needed was the fun of swimming out to the ship instead of joining the really tired trekkers taking the launch.

Pace yourself: the tortoise can beat the hare.

Chapter Nine

COMPANIONSHIP

Travellers vary: families, married couples, unmarried couples, singles including widows and widowers, pensioners, adventurers, workers and career business professionals. Some look for fun and relief from daily business pressures, on their annual holidays. The newly retired are in a change-of-life state, seeking fresh horizons. Itchy footed adventurers and dreamers have been waiting half a lifetime to see a far-off land. With rare exceptions (see Chapter Ten) they have one thought in common: they do not want to travel alone.

COMPANIONABLE SINGLES

Individuals who are uncomfortable with strangers, but reluctant to travel alone, should seek a friend or friends from social groups or the workplace. Or a relative might be asked to travel as a companion, in an adventure of mutual interest. Arrangements of this kind can seldom be worked out and made jointly, as we have recommended to couples. Here, one person completes the research and, before booking, will ask about for a companion who can arrange a holiday at the same time. A friend of many years could be tempted to join the adventure. In the end, three or more may like the idea.

There is a risk in 'tiny group' travel. Two individuals sometimes find it hard to decide what to do for the day, where to dine for the evening or even what to wear. A formula has it that three persons quadruple the problem, while four to six travelling together so magnify the decision processes that a dictator is required.

With or without a dictator, there is the 'disgruntled' factor. One person simply doesn't want to go along with the crowd, which causes annoying confrontations. Thus four good friends who have played poker or whist together for years are now at odds with each other. Think about it and discuss it, well before confirming joint plans. The group must foresee the problem with a sense of humour, and early on devise a system to beat it. One easy solution is similar to a friendly poker game: each player gains status in turn as 'the dealer' who selects the 'hand' to be played. Rotating the decision-making really does make a game out of a problem.

TAKING POT LUCK WITH A SMALL GROUP

Six to eight people can make an ideal tour group. After agreeing on a travel destination, your agent suggests a certain trip, restricted to eight; and they would meet at the airport or boat. Let us say that four are in couples, you and three others are singles, and ages range from 30 to 60.

Travelling in 'double occupancy' means that you will join with one of the other singles to share a room throughout the trip. To some people this is a great opportunity to make a new friend with an interest in the chosen kind of travel. Others fear being 'doubled' with a stranger, even in the interests of economy. What if the new companion has some unfortunate habit?

In another group some members would not like to travel with other people's small children. Couples can take early exception to a hanging-on single, or to another couple who are 'thrilled to be with them'. It is embarrassing constantly to dodge unwanted companions.

Therefore, when undertaking small group travel, it is important to know explicitly who the companions are going to be, in person or by description.

A good travel bureau will arrange a pre-booking plus pairing of singles meeting, ostensibly to discuss destination information, but actually helping the probable group to gel. If the agent doesn't offer, it would be a good idea to suggest such a get-together. One single lady friend of ours always contacts the person she is to be teamed with, face-to-face or by phone – far in advance of the departure date. Tastes, smoking habits and age difference can all make or break the adventure.

Travelling as a couple is less problematical; a single always has some trepidation before meeting the strangers who will be close companions for many days.

☞ **Personal Experience**
My wife and I booked a seven-day adventure to the tiny Himalayan country of Bhutan. We joined a group of six single ladies, ages 60 to 80, gathered from various directions. A mini van with driver-guide appeared, and the eight passengers spent the next week in very close proximity.

There were annoyances such as the constant shouting to the guide to stop for pictures, bathroom competition and 'when do we eat' distractions. Meal times were exactly structured which made sure that the party fed together – though we much prefer dining in private. A mountain-climbing expedition, partly on horseback, became difficult because we naturally took responsibility for the ladies unfamiliar with horses. Whenever we sought privacy we felt guilty, as if we were sneaking off by ourselves to shop or whatever.

The most difficult part for us was the constant close-companionship of the group. It narrowed our perspectives. We like to meet local people, develop some intimacy with the guides, and explore villages.

Our chagrin was magnified when we discovered that group travel had not been necessary. By contacting the tourist department of Bhutan in Thimbu, we could easily have arranged an independent trip at no higher cost. Our great friend, the travel agent, was misinformed or deliberately misinformed us.

Lesson and recommendation: extensive research will reveal alternatives.

The bright side of small-group travel is that, with the right mix, the ambience becomes family-like. Waiting for stragglers happens less. Closeness makes people far more aware of inconvenience to the group. Humour replaces annoyance. Minor changes of plan are easily agreed upon if weather interferes or a diverting side trip appears. We would choose a small rather than a large group whenever possible.

LARGE-GROUP TRAVEL

A sizeable group is necessarily regimented. Shepherding two score or more people is difficult for the guides; that is, keeping up to 30 diverse people happy, safe and well fed. Their charges have paid large sums for the package and expect good value. Constant counts to ensure that everyone is aboard are annoying;

more so is waiting for the two people who are always late or have to go back for a lost article. Particular seats on the bus are objects of contention. The first row is best for visibility; commandeering it causes resentment. The guide is accused of favouring certain persons to the irritation of others.

Enjoyment of the trip can be clouded by the interplay of social problems generated by a group of strangers vying for recognition. A misunderstanding of arrangements, or a particularly unfortunate occurrence at the breakfast table, can take time away from viewing the scenery. People feel put out instead of uplifted.

More time is spent queuing when a large-group leader must organise his charges long before departure. Mountains of luggage need to be gathered and dispatched. Milling about accelerates annoyance when the weather is too hot, too cold or too wet.

Large groups present their own set of pros and cons. They are more cumbersome to take part in, but have the advantage of anonymity. Singles can pay extra for single rooms or request a switch of roommates; and couples or subgroups can divert themselves without causing attention.

Enough of the possible negatives. Perennial optimists will swear that the usual misfortunes will not happen to them, and I agree. For they keep their sense of humour, pay no attention to the detractors and look on the bright side.

On that bright side, they realise that most large groups are of like-minded people organised by a school, a business or professional association, or some other fraternity. Or they have all been attracted by the tour's special character. Its members will take the opportunity, away from the daily grind, to enjoy relaxed companionship while discussing professional or recreational topics. The interplay extends into exchanges about non-common factors such as each others' professions, skills or talents.

Small circles – or cliques – develop. Sometimes these closer friendships survive to future excursions, and beyond.

SUMMARY

Companionship provides the opportunity to enlarge the scope of personal relationships. Each individual or couple makes of it what they will. It is sensible to conduct relationships to enhance the pleasure of your tour. Don't hesitate to correct any uncomfortable situation from the outset. Group leaders are well attuned to such problems. They will switch your roommate or your seating. In an extreme case they will allow you to detach from the group. You have advanced good money for a rare experience in a congenial ambience. You should insist on good value for your investment.

Chapter Ten

WOMEN TRAVELLING ALONE

The exception to the notion that everyone wants company is the woman who aspires to the exquisite freedom of travelling on her own – of being the quintessential Independent Traveller. This chapter is dedicated to her, and to her accomplishments without tour group or companion.

THE VENTURESOME SPOUSE

Some women, though happily married, prefer to travel alone. Business or professional women, travelling solo on duty, accustom themselves to certain comforts and requirements provided by major hotels. For privacy they use special executive floors, each with a concierge on hand, and there enjoy continental breakfasts plus pre-evening cocktail hours. Articles and books on the subject have long lists of do's and don'ts which the novice pleasure-traveller can learn from.

According to the lore, there are men – gentle and kind husbands or partners – who are horrible to travel with. Leaving home, and spending money in the process, is foreign to their nature. Travel turns them into disgruntled rogues. In a strange environment, they react obstreperously to the change from their home routine. "It's 6:30: why can't we have dinner now instead of 8:00? We always eat at 6:30. This place is awful, I couldn't even get a three-minute egg made right this morning. The maid moved my shaver. It looks like rain today, I think we ought to go home." Trivialities, aggravated by unfamiliar surroundings, destroy the entire sweet aroma of the adventure.

So: leave him at home.

THE ENCAPSULED SINGLE

Many women live independent lives. Never-married women (and men) are accepted and respected in today's world. Professional and business careers encourage single-living amongst achievers. Widowhood and divorces send people back to an individual's lifestyle. Often, however, there are children, still at home and involved in the daily pattern of existence.

Women in these situations may feel encapsuled, caught in the web of career, family, well-meaning friends and the style of life expected of them. To join fellow travellers in a tour group is to transfer from one cage to another. Tour groups invariably have more single women than couples. Being tied to a routine, even in a foreign country, resembles too much the predictable as endured at home. The challenge is to avoid fetters, go off alone, see the grazing lands of the Rich and Famous.

Escapism it may be. But it allows one to recharge the independent batteries, take an overview of one's life, imagine changes, and perhaps use time to reorganise. Treat it more like a holiday than the cure for a malady. What is wrong with wanting to concoct a little fun and toss some new experiences into the salad of travel? Married or single, woman or man, we all get in a rut and can use a new perspective.

By the time this year's escape has prompted next year's programme, no independent woman will need this chapter to tell her how to relax and/or venture overseas. As for details, a knowledgeable concierge will arrange a tour of the city and tickets for the ballet. He will advise about restaurants that cater comfortably for single women, and book a special table.

PHYSICAL SECURITY AND COMFORT

Whatever their age, women worry about being accosted or taken advantage of, especially abroad. Crime is over-publicised almost everywhere. There is anxiety about being charged too much in a taxi, or coerced into an unearned tip, about one's purse being stolen in a busy street – and a hundred greater or lesser disasters. These fears are warranted. The long-planned adventure can be spoiled or ruined, or worse.

This list of do's and don'ts comes from seasoned women business travellers. Take it with you, *and scan the list every morning*, for items which could relate to the day's plan:
• Use inconspicuous luggage, duffels preferably.
• Never bring cases or bags heavier than you can easily lift.
• Two small pieces of luggage are better than one large one.
• Ask for side-row aircraft seating as far forward as possible.
• Put make-up and a change of clothes in the carry-on bag.
• Use a hand trolley for carry-on luggage.
• Carry an ample handbag with a shoulder strap and closed top.
• Wear a minimum of jewellery.
• Put valuables in a safe in the hotel.
• Empty the safe before the final departure.
• Have passport and tickets readily available at the airport.
• Keep a pad and pen handy to make notes during journeys.

- Acquire some (small) local currency before you need it.
- Spend small notes; at the airport exchange any large ones left.
- Never share a taxi.
- When out at night, pre-arrange a return taxi.
- Tell the concierge where you'll be and when to expect you.
- Telephone the concierge if you will return significantly later.
- Re-confirm departure flights and your next hotel arrival time.
- Leave more than ample time for airport departure.
- Dress for physical comfort.
- Never carry anything (however small) for any stranger.

Most of these suggestions appear in one way or another elsewhere in the text. They are concentrated here for the single woman traveller because lone travel is a cause of worry and, often, confusion. Airport check-ins, luggage handling, and customs and immigration procedures are disconcerting. Even the busy crowds are unsettling. You may be tired when you arrive in an unfamiliar country, perhaps later in the small hours than expected. The regulations, the luggage claim, and eventually the strange hotel: taken separately, each can be coped with; it is the cumulative effect that calls for this list and the careful organisation it should ensure. Thus prepared, you should be free from crises.

A note pad in the bag is handy to write down the restaurant a stewardess has recommended or a point of particular interest mentioned in the flight magazine or newspaper. It is invaluable for recording thoughts that surface when you are trying to sleep.

Dress comfortably. Carry a purse with a side pocket reserved for easy-access travel documents and a top that closes. Skirts allow more scrunching-around, and toilet comfort. Shoes that can slip back on when long flights swell the feet, and a sweater to combat the air-conditioning, add to your sense of being smart-cosy. Anticipate the arrival climate in selecting travel garments.

Wear a minimum of jewellery. Costume and *faux* gems have

their place in travelling. Many hotel rooms are equipped with *en suite* safes, and all have a secure lock-box system near the cashier.

Re-pack your luggage and empty the safe the night before your departure, to make leaving less hectic in the morning. Arrange a wake-up call for an early morning check-out; travelling alters waking habits. When you are sure you have everything, look again – under the bed, in drawers, behind the bathroom door, in and on the night table. Leaving a favourite lipstick or undergarment is very annoying, but not worth the effort to recover.

Leave the normal purse or shoulder bag in the hotel for daily excursions or beach visits. Buy a waist pouch for the needs of the day. Passport, tickets and traveller's cheques remain in the safe. You only need your day's cash, a credit card, quick make-up items, handkerchiefs or tissues, and cigarettes if you smoke. Thus you won't have to put a bag down while trying on a new dress or having lunch. Street-wise rip-off characters won't be tempted to grab and run. A bag hanging on the back of a chair in a busy restaurant is a theft invitation. Caution develops routine security habits, which replace constant fear.

Obtain some currency of the country you are visiting, in advance, for arrival tips and taxi fares. Almost all airport concourses have money changers, but arrival processes are confusing enough already.

Never allow anyone you don't know to share a taxi, regardless of the supposed emergency. Similarly, do not accept a ride from a stranger met on the plane. Con artists are often a sweet-looking elderly couple, an efficient-looking executive male with attaché case – or even uniformed, such as airline or military officers. Con men don't look like con men. There are no exceptions to the no-share rule. The taxi driver will support your demand for privacy; if not, get out and take another cab. But don't forget to retrieve your luggage.

Tie a bright-coloured ribbon onto the handle of your luggage, making it easier to identify as it comes round the baggage carousel. If a porter is available, it is well worth a two-buck tip to have him take your luggage and you to the taxi or limousine queue. With a bill in your hand he will wait until you are properly ensconced in the right vehicle. There is no worry or confusion at most airports, but some can be threatening and/or chaotic.

Before leaving the hotel for shopping or other jaunts, ask the concierge to write the destination for the taxi in the local vernacular. Ask the doorman, while you wait for a taxi, to relay this address to the driver. Make sure the driver knows the precise destination. It is both acceptable and advisable to ask the probable cost of the trip.

For single women, it's especially important to travel light. Use the smaller duffel bags that weigh no more than 10 kilos when filled. The normal airline hold-baggage allowance is 20 kilos (44 pounds). When charged, the excess is often steep. What you are permitted to carry on varies – and could be dangerously heavy. It should contain a change of clothes suitable for arrival, and cosmetic requirements in addition to the absolute necessities. A lightweight 'trolley' or 'cart' is very convenient for the long walks down airport wings.

ASSERTING ONESELF

A single woman traveller in a strange city and an impersonal hotel can feel inhibited. Feminists insist the single woman can and should exercise the same prerogatives as a single man. Enter the lounge for a twilight two-for-one cocktail – or a port before retiring – if that is what you would like. You are not looking for company; you want to write some cards, perhaps, or at least get out of the claustrophobic room. Carry a book with you, or an impressive newspaper, to ward off the stares of males who might assume you were looking for company. Starting a conversation with a stranger, male or female, is at your discretion.

Eating alone in one's room is depressing for some. Use the informal coffee shop for plebeian dining amongst the crowd. However, when you would prefer fine dining, wine and formal service, don't deny yourself the pleasure. Inform the *maître d'* that you prefer a semi-private table facing the room, away from any large or noisy groups. A snooty male chauvinist may offer you a table next to the service door or on top of the waiter's section. Look around the room and tell him which place you have in mind. If not satisfied, leave. All hotels have service questionnaires in the rooms, as the staff well know; it is amazing how quickly the sneer turns into a smile and superb service, when you ask for the name and title of an unhelpful employee.

Tipping seems to be part of the male psyche. Men tend to over-tip to impress their female companions and, hopefully, to be recognised next time. Women not used to travelling alone are often uncomfortable with the procedure. When the bill includes a service charge, there is no need to add anything unless you have genuinely enjoyed special attention. Friendly snack shops and cafes, or a porter who takes extra time to show you how to operate all the room gadgets and provides some personal insight to the hotel and city – these have earned a token of your thanks. A taxi driver who drives carefully, talks or doesn't talk as it suits you, and helps with your luggage, deserves extra coinage or the rounding up to a 20-unit note of an 18.60 meter reading.

☛ **Travel Tip**

If you disagree with the driver over a taxi fare on reaching your hotel, ask the doorman or hotel greeter to sort it out. In other instances of probable rip-off, carefully note down the driver's name and taxi number, plus the date, time and location. Again, this simple act can have a marvellous influence on the perpetrator.

Caution

Among the freedoms of Independent Travel is the freedom to form friendships, probably short-term, with women or men. Different nationalities add to the interest but do not change the rules of the game. If you are a businesswoman, you will know that any opportunity that arises for you to transfer an asset is a sign that the friend is bogus. Men who make their living in this way delight in breaking hearts. They will keep up the pretence, by letter or telephone, when they know they will see no more of the victim or her money.

Chapter Eleven

DE-SHOCKING THE COSTS

HAVE A GOOD HOLIDAY?

Package tour operators make it look easy with the luring advertisement: '21 days in Hawaii, Los Angeles, San Francisco, Denver – including a glorious three days in Las Vegas – for US$2,100.' We have discussed this in Chapter Four. All you have to do is examine the plan, make sure you like it, put down the money, take a few hundred extra for eating and the inevitable at Vegas. When you get home, the shocking overrun on your credit card reveals that you've spent another US$2,100. Where did the money go? Is travelling really worth it?

Costs are always shocking. Even wealthy people fret at the price of a first-class air passage at several hundred dollars per hour of cushy seats and fancy food. We, the great middle income group of society, must guard our dollars from the predators to get the most enjoyment value. The way to make sense out of spending the bundle that, alas, we are going to spend is to estimate a realistic budget and then keep the opportunists away from the wallet. By using some common sense and rules of thumb, we can still have a time that justifies its cost.

TRAVEL BUDGET

To get over any danger of costs stirring up your heart problems, try this travel-budget plan. Package tourists have a basic outlay in the booking agent's price. The 21-day 'United States Fling' on the previous page includes 'all land costs and free American Breakfast'. All you need do is add in the air fare and subtract the total from the maximum you can afford to spend – and divide what remains by the number of whole days (probably 20). The result is your daily average budget for the extras.

Independent Travellers have a more complicated problem. The return air fare for the itinerary is the same, but the land costs must be estimated.

A Package

A couple starts the tabulation with 2 x 2,100 = US$4,200. Wherever you are, Deluxe Economy meal costs depend mainly on your eating and drinking habits. For example, $35 for dinner, $25 for lunch, and $15 for snacks equals $75; but add another $25 if you like a couple of beers during the day and a bottle of wine for dinner, and the amount rounds out to $100. Economisers may skip lunch and the drinks, to shop for souvenirs or enjoy a massage. Rounding up, you can estimate $6,500 for the three-week adventure for two. A similar tour to quieter places nearer home, more Economy than Deluxe, can easily reduce that amount by one third.

Thus, so long as you hold to average daily 'extras' of $100 (or $75), you will know from the outset what the holiday will cost.

The Independent Traveller

The computation is the same as above, except for the basic travel cost. Though the return air fare will not change, you should in either case seek a bargain, as a later chapter will explain. The level of accommodation is controlled by the chosen style of the travelling pair. Large cities have hotel rooms from US$125, while motels can be under $50. A cafe breakfast or lunch is considerably less than a hotel buffet. Splurge for dinner at a fine restaurant, sometimes; have a pizza delivered to the motel room at others. The daily cost of food for two can be regulated up or down between $50 and $150 – giving a high average of $125, say, and a low of $75.

It is the same with the rooms. You will arrive at a similar budget for the 20-night holiday, and a target average overnight bill. Here too you will go for luxury where it beckons, and help the average with a bargain when that offers.

For travel in Asia we lump together the sleeping and eating variables, and budget $150 a day for the pair of us. Journeys within Asia, including side trips, are extra. This is the standard we call Deluxe Economy – using four- or five-star hotels but spending less on food and extra 'extras'. The trick is to buy the least expensive facilities at the finest establishments. If you cannot resist your bottle of Chardonnay with a fancy dinner every night, change the estimate to $200/$250 per day. Our Circle Pacific ticket (see Chapter Five) adds US$5,000 to the total.

Travel Axiom: The Longer You Travel, the Less You Spend

This realistic assumption is justified by the spread of ticket costs over six weeks or two months instead of 21 days. But longer stays in one place can reduce room and food costs per diem, also. The hotel will give you a better room rate; and as you settle in you will tend to eat snacks, in your room or elsewhere, for lunch and/ or breakfast; you will also find yourself stepping down to the cheaper colds and salads at buffet dinners, without going hungry.

You now have, for package and Independent Travellers, estimates of the amount necessary to finance the adventure. Add a reserve of 10% for over-spending, and then work out where the money is coming from. Some people keep one credit card exclusively for annual holiday travel. They ignore the bank's requirement of a modicum each month and pay one-twelfth regardless, to clear the debt in time for the next year's odyssey. The guilty feeling lessens if you compare it to the necessity of a rent or mortgage payment on your home or car. The key word is necessity. Enjoying a fine holiday adventure each year is as indispensable to life as owning a residence and an automobile.

Big cities like Singapore, Hong Kong, New York, London and Paris cost more; fine small resorts in (say) Portugal, Malaysia or the Philippines, much less. Back-packing youngsters do it for under US$25 a day, but elders need a little more physical comfort. In northern Europe Deluxe Economy is expensive; in the United States and Australia, middling; and in parts of Asia, very modest. For two, a daily average could range from US$100 to US$500. Initial overseas flights vary with distance and the package you choose.

Chapter Eight has tips on saving money while getting the most out of the system. Consider the money you save as prolonging the adventure. Some of that advice is repeated in the following sections, re-stated for your convenience in this budget context.

Budget for the maximum; never delude yourself with a minimum.

SAVING MONEY
Your dollar stretches when you watch all money transactions.

Changing Currency
This is a mystery to the unwary. Keep in mind that it is a profit-

making business for hotels, money changers, bank exchange services and credit card companies. One per cent is an average handling charge by the banks and major card companies. So be it, as long as the exchange is calculated from the international rates. These are quoted in most national and the bigger local newspapers.

Credit Cards

These provide the best system for spending in foreign countries; the rates are controlled and in order. Conversion is customarily 1% over the published international rate on the day the card company receives the voucher. The system of international cards is so electronically efficient that you may obtain a cash advance almost anywhere in the world in a few minutes. No worry about running out of currency or carrying a lot of cash or traveller's cheques. Transport systems, hotels, restaurants and commercial theatres all readily accept credit cards; large to medium shops do likewise, except in remote areas.

In many countries, travel agents may charge extra for card purchases. You can avoid this, or at least reduce it, by obtaining cash with the credit card.

Traveller's Cheques

This form of flexibility is now little used by the experienced traveller. If you are a worrier and careless with personal effects, you should insure against loss. The issuing company benefits, on a principle opposite to that of the credit card: they have the use of your money until you cash or spend their cheques.

American Express has a great advertising line aimed at keeping unused cheques in your pocket for the next trip. What a way to make money: sell people your cheques, charge them and then tell them not to cash in. Mind you, the customer who prudently buys more than enough of these things would lose in another way through cashing the surplus and then paying another percent to purchase them back from the issuing bank the next year – and at least another 1% off the international rate on cashing them abroad.

Meanwhile the holder must keep track of the cheques used and retain the register list separately. If a loss occurs the company will require to be told which cheques were used where, and the numbers on the remaining block.

Street Money Changers

If you know the international rate beforehand, you will usually find the small-shop (or even open-air) changers very fair as well as convenient. On longer trips, we often change currency with them for the next country on our itinerary.

Hotels and Banks

While they may look more reliable, hotels will take up to 5% more from you than will the man behind the street counter. If you must change money in your hotel, change the minimum. Banks often charge a fee or commission as well. Ask or look for a 'No commission' sign at the changer or in the bank. Hotels and banks post major exchange rates in their lobbies for easy reference: in the former, look for the spread between buying and selling figures.

Airport Money Changers

Perhaps taking advantage of a strategic position, changers in airports usually give less favourable rates than those in shopping streets and malls. So don't change much on the way in or out – but the absence of a commission could influence you the other way.

☛ Personal Experience

Sometimes it seems impossible to change money or make purchases at or near the official rate. On a recent visit to the

Philippines, the international rate was almost P29 to US$1, the hotel offered P24, and stores exchanged for P25. One travel agent quoted me P1,400 for a particular side trip, and then asked US$66 for the same service. Even at the high average of P25, he was skimming P250, making it almost 20% off the international rate. It's tough to fight because you are in their country. In such cases, we politely turn down any surcharged service and explain why. Try to pay everything you can with your credit card.

☛ **Travel Tip**
For pocket cash, check with the money changers in one country for the exchange rate of the next. If you know the international rate and are being offered only a point off, get the cash before you leave. If you have money left over at the end of your next stay, use it towards the hotel bill. But keep enough for the taxi and airport departure tax. Also, when the itinerary goes through more than one country, you can change leftover currency to that of the next. This means you only get clipped once on the exchange.

If one of your party has a problem with calculating, make a little card with pre-computed exchange rates both ways for useful denominations of your currency against the local. It makes for easy reference when shopping.

Money exchange and its problems can be annoying and time consuming, and so distract one from enjoying the adventure. Prepare ahead, and there will be no such distraction. Moreover you will be saved from the 'corner clippers', as we call them.

Prepayment
Paying ahead for travel arrangements may make you feel secure, but it means the money comes out of your bank account long before you use the purchased item. Tours often require a major deposit – or all of the price – weeks or months in advance. For

our six-month odysseys, we pay as we go except for the basic air ticket. Thus our expenses are paid on our return. If there are interest charges, they mainly begin much later than with full prepayment.

For tours, push the travel agent to hold off until the last possible time of payment. Agents need to collect in advance to make sure of their commission. Independent Travellers should do as little advance paying as possible. The problem is the difficulty of getting a refund if you don't or can't use all you paid for.

To claim a refund, you must apply to the person or company that took your deposit in the first place. That means the agent. If you wish to change hotels, the prepayment is irrecoverable, which is very frustrating. Therefore make reservations yourself by fax or phone, guarantee the first night with your credit card and pay when you leave the hotel. Provided you give 48 hours notice of non-arrival or early departure, neither the hotel nor the credit card company could defend charging for more than the guaranteed period.

There is an interesting phenomenon in hotel bookings. If you reserve for a week, guaranteeing the first night, and leave after two days, no one says a word. The cashier takes your money for the two nights and cheerfully waves you off. Extending your stay is rarely a problem if you're travelling independently. One room in a hotel with 300 or 600 is 'always' available.

Some small and exclusive resorts however will impose their own rules if you want to stay during fully-booked periods. For example: Qamea Beach Club in Fiji, with only 10 *bure*, is soft-hearted and will accept a direct reservation with a credit card guarantee; while the hardened souls at Lizard Island, Great Barrier Reef, want half with the booking and the balance weeks before you get there.

Remember the traveller's axiom: "It is my money, and I'm the customer."

☛ **Travel Tip**
On average, the cheapest way to pay for travel is to charge your credit card and pay within the 'no-service-charge' deadline.

TIPPING

Squander or conserve. You can be a big tipper or save some dollars to spend in a better way. Tipping is an annoyance because customs vary from place to place. Most large hotel chains and restaurants charge '+ +' for a total called 'nett'. This is a 10% (or 15%) service charge (employee benefits supposedly) and a 5% (or 10%) sales tax (government benefit).

When the tip is automatically included and the service is normal we don't add anything. If the bell hop has to struggle with an overload of luggage and renders extra service in settling us in, we do slip him a dollar or so. A helpful taxi driver normally gets the small change left over from the fare.

In some areas – Hong Kong and the US for example – everyone expects to be tipped. Singapore reverses the trend by deliberately requesting no tipping in major hotels (though your credit card chit will thoughtfully leave open the chance to defy that request). Australians consider it demeaning and don't expect it. The same principle should apply universally: tipping is a reward for extra service, not a device to help the employer's payroll.

The new electronic twist to the tipping tail is confusing to some travellers. Automatic processing of credit cards in restaurants uses a form that has a space marked 'tip' on top of (though literally below) the total which includes '+ +'. Don't be browbeaten, ignore it. Whatever you do, avoid giving a percentage of the bill and of the pluses... If a waiter has earned a real thank you, leave a sum in cash on the table. The classic system of making sure the person you want to reward gets the tip, is to conceal it in a goodbye handshake. Old-fashioned but effective.

COMMUNICATION

For Independent Travellers, direct contact with the accommodation at various destinations is very important and easy. Whether booking with a travel agent or doing it yourself, it is comforting to have address information and names of staff during planning and before arrival. Contact and reconfirmation of itinerary while on the way are important.

There are the usual methods of telephone and mail plus the newest boon to travellers, facsimile service by telephone wire. Fax is so prevalent today that all but the most rural of the people you communicate with are equipped. If you have no office and your home does not have the facility, local secretarial services and most post offices make them available. Charges vary, especially for incoming foreign messages, so shop around. In small communities the local book and office-supplies store usually offers a fax service.

For long advance planning, mail is sufficient to establish a contact, get the desired information, and follow up. Fax is better for more urgent reservations. Date changes are better handled by phone call with written fax confirmation. A verbal discussion can resolve differences in time of arrival and temporary fully-booked problems. (You can dial direct from most hotels, but ask beforehand about hotel surcharges.)

The same is true of communication with your home whilst away. Postcards take 10 days to two weeks from the most distant countries. Fax messages, if you have good points of contact, are instant though not as personal. Phone calls are often difficult because of time differences and availability of the other party. The fax line stands ready 24 hours a day like a good soldier. Send the family a fax on arrival at each destination, with the hotel number and the time difference – and whether to add or subtract.

To facilitate telephone calls, we include in the 'arrived' fax the best time to call calculated in the home zone time. For instance, we're normally in our room before breakfast and thus available to receive a call if necessary. Most overseas calls are cheaper from home, and contact is readily made. Advise your fax correspondent to be sure to use your name. The Singapore Shangri-La had some difficulty one year delivering a fax addressed to Dear Mom and Dad.

Watch the Costs

Fax and telephone costs vary considerably. It is a profit-making enterprise for most hotels, and they often add from 10% to 40% to the actual charges. Some back-breakers charge by the page, others use a minimum cost plus time used. Be sure to ask for costs before using overseas communication services.

Access to the worldwide AT&T service is unique and low cost. Special facilities (now expanding to other parts of the world) are available for travelling US residents. With the proper card, call a pre-specified number in the foreign country, connecting immediately with an AT&T operator as a collect call. You punch in the number desired and the various card and code numbers. It is billed directly to your own number at local rates. Enquire from your phone service company before you leave, about any special communication services available when out of your country.

The old cliché 'It's a small world' was never more apt than in referring to modern communication systems.

AIR TICKETS

Flight is the major cost reflected in the price of tour packages. The vendor can control hotel portions by the quality and what each hotel will throw into the deal. Thus if you are designing your own package, the first thing to determine is the flight cost. Then you can work in the accommodation and hire car or side trips.

The problem is, prices vary within the same airline and

between booking methods. An intricate web of special dates, times of the year, days of the week, half-fare and frequent-flier arrangements is ultimately confusing.

The choices are:

- Contact the airline direct. Reserve the package; then ask a travel agency to write the ticket.
- Contact the airline and buy the ticket in their office.
- Persuade your agency to shop for the best rate and supply the ticket.
- Shop carefully round discount ticket ('bucket') shops, but with a wary eye on arrangements to deliver the tickets to you.

My favourite system is to call the airline, obtain a quoted rate and flight information, and then see whether travel agencies can produce a better plan.

HIRE CAR

There are special rates for advance booking by international operators like Hertz, Avis, Budget, etc. Local car rental agencies provide a variety of rates depending on limitations and drop-off charges. The international companies are easy to check on. Your hometown office will provide the information. Discover local rental car agencies at your destination by questioning the hotel concierge, reading counter brochures and telephoning Yellow Pages listings on arrival. Hotel personnel get a commission from the rental car vendor if they place the order. Call some of the local people to discover any variation in prices for direct booking.

Competition forces the local companies to offer better prices, sometimes half those of the international ones. As ever, you must check all the details and ask the hotel about reliability. Local companies do not have as many drop-off points, if any, should you want to divest the vehicle at the other end of the trip. There are always two ways to buy the service. One is unlimited mileage, the other is per mile. Go over a map with the clerk to determine the distances you will probably travel. The good companies will compute the cost both ways on your return and charge you the lesser amount. You will also pay for all petrol.

Checklist
- Specific vehicle desired (for uniform comparison of hirers).
- Unlimited mileage, or base charge plus mileage?
- Drop-off charge?
- Drop-off points?
- What if I need repairs or service?
- Extra charges per diem, for insurance or whatever?
- Credit card payment?
- Limits of use, such as unpaved roads, etc.?

TRAVEL INSURANCE

Travel industry people tend to agree that North America, Switzerland, Hong Kong and Japan are notorious for being the most expensive places in which to have an accident or fall ill. However, Thomas Cook's travel agency points out that it can be just as costly in third world countries, despite the likely absence of modern facilities.

Some experienced embassy officers advise that if you can't afford an insurance policy, you can't afford to travel. Some booking agencies offer insurance cover along with an extensive tour, or include it in the total price. Thomas Cook quotes three categories of cover: budget, standard and super plus – ranging in cost from US$175 to US$225 for a family on a 21-day trip.

These policies will include cancellation-of-trip clauses, whether by the traveller or the tour operator. Agencies have gone bankrupt while their clients were in the middle of a tour. Transport and accommodation were therefore unpaid, creating great havoc in the travel plans. Prepaid travel notwithstanding, the travellers were left stranded in a foreign city, and forced to pay (again) for – and make – arrangements to finish the journey and return home.

Each airline will have a policy giving cover for aircraft accidents, but effective only on its leg of the journey. American Express has an automatic accidental death policy purchase system (for 75 US cents) in effect whenever you buy your ticket with their card. Other card companies have similar free or low cost, but often severely restricted, cover.

Health and Accident Policies
Medical/health insurance taken out in your own country will probably not cover expenditure outside territorial limits. You must consider specific travel policies if you want cover abroad. As with any insurance purchase, the customer must evaluate the possible risks and then read the fine print.

A travel policy will cover:
• Trip cancellation.
• Very limited medical services.
• Accidental death or loss of limb.
• Emergency evacuation.
• Repatriation of remains, in case of death.
• Lost or stolen luggage.

A typical 1994 premium would be US$60 for a 31-day family trip. Extended excursions are covered by a surcharge per diem which may make the policy non-cost-effective. Study the exact cover limits and charges before you buy.

Elderly people are susceptible to heart problems, falls and fractures that require hospital treatment and/or expert medical care. Younger persons are prone to sports related accidents like the proverbial broken leg on a ski trip. Scuba divers can buy relevant cover on an annual basis whatever the location, as may racing-car drivers and parachutists.

The important part is the small print, where the exceptions and exclusions appear.

118

Homeowners' and Worldwide General Policies

Many 'home and effects' (or 'house and contents') policies cover loss worldwide of personal possessions within the limits stated. They can include luggage, jewellery and equipment plus expenses incurred in connection with the loss. Expensive individual items must be specifically listed and appraised, for which you will pay. Look up your policy and check for the exceptions. Take these into consideration when purchasing a travel policy. Double coverage will seldom pay double if you do have a loss. The primary insurer pays first, and the secondary will cover what's left only.

Which insurance company is providing the cover? Make sure it is well known and reputable. This is up to the selling agent to prove to your satisfaction. Insurance policies sold by the big travel companies (Thomas Cook, American Express, etc.) obviously have substantial backing. Unknowns are suspect. If the agent does not satisfy or evades your curiosity, buy a policy direct from a known insurance company.

☛ **Observation**

Like travel agents, money changers and the many other professionals with whom travellers deal, insurance companies and the vendors of their policies are in business to make profits. You insure your life because, for your dependants, it is irreplaceable. Under much the same compulsion, you insure the house you live in, if you own it. But if you owned 10 houses it would usually be more profitable to stand the risks of damage and destruction than to pay premiums for a company to stand the 10-fold risks. It is simpler, and on average cheaper, not to insure against misfortunes which would cost you – but by no means ruin you. This, you might say, is a near relation of Deluxe Economy.

'Simpler' is an over-simplification, of course. It is true insofar as *laissez-faire* cuts out paper work, which includes the writing of premium cheques. It might still be true when the gamble does not pay off, for whatever you may have to do to restore the position, it won't include making and pursuing a claim. But there will be times when a big organisation will do for you what you cannot easily do yourself, whether the claim relates to travel or domestic disasters.

Checklist
If you haven't already got it, you need to investigate cover for:
- Health care abroad, including accidents to body and limb.
- Medical evacuation to hospital and home.
- Trip cancellation.
- Failure of vendor to complete contract.
- Loss of luggage and personal effects.
- Accidents in vehicles or non-scheduled aircraft.
- Compensation for interruption of journey.
- Extra accidental death cover.

Chapter Twelve

SHOCKING FOODS

Eating a new and unusual gastronomic delight is one of the rare pleasures of life. Enjoyment of a fruit never tasted before is an adventure, though not everyone likes the tropical durian. There must be a taste for excitement in the soul if one is to sample the range of food preparations around the world.

Travellers with simpler tastes will find it easier to enjoy more of their familiar food today than ever before. The prevalence of international food franchises means you can have your fix with a double-whammy burger in Beijing, Moscow or wherever. Local clones of these chains multiply the familiar food menus. You can get fried chicken almost anywhere.

At the other extreme are gourmets who look for fine dining

and rare wines wherever they go. Five-star hotels have fancy dress dining rooms, elegant service, prestige menus, champagne, caviar – and Swiss-trained chefs preparing *haute cuisine*.

Between these two groups are the rest of us: ordinary mortals who like the thrill of new tastes at fair prices, and the fun of variety. As age comes upon us, seven-course dinners are reduced to six, then five and eventually three courses in the interest of better health. We snack more and over-stuff less as physical comfort and good sense overcome greed.

WHERE TO EAT?

Always available in reserve is the average hotel coffee house – not necessarily your hotel's – with a varied menu of soups, salads, pasta, grills, local fare or three-course set dinners. It is easier to use that facility when tired from arrival or after a long day touring. When you have the energy, it is fun to stroll down the fashionable artery of a city like Singapore with an appetite but no set plans for dinner. Look at menus of a dozen different restaurants, peer inside some of them, and then go for what most tempts the palate. Unexpectedly finding a Mövenpick with a Swiss menu of *raclette* and a crisply fresh salad bar, plus a sweet counter from which to take an apple strudel back to the hotel – that is a successful treasure hunt.

In cities with mainly scattered restaurants, consult the telephone book, and ask the concierge and the doorman to recommend eating places. Breakfast away from the hotel is often an interesting and rewarding adventure. Try the central shopping and business district where coffee shops and takeaways abound. Office and retail business people know where to go. Pick the busiest one you can find where you have to queue to get a cappuccino and fresh pastry.

Before an evening dinner, take the trouble to call the suggested restaurant yourself. A few minutes on the phone enquiring about food styles and prices, and gauging the voice-welcome, will tell you what to expect. Try two or three for the most interesting response. When booking, ask the name of the person you are talking to and on arrival try to meet him or her. A compliment on the telephone demeanour may produce instant rapport, because everyone's ego loves to be polished. Now that you are old friends, a nicer table, food suggestions and a positive atmosphere go a long way to make your evening special.

In some of our favourite cities, the dining variety in our hotel is so marvellous that we don't bother to go out. Another factor is the length of sojourn in one location, which brings on a certain contentment with familiar dining. A pleasant dinner, chosen from an excellently varied menu, invites return visits. Staff get to know your tastes, willingly agree to prepare dishes especially to suit, and often suggest unusual items not on the menu. Variety is said to be the spice of life; to enjoy this spice in a continuing comfortable ambience and a contented glow is all the more satisfying. Keep a note in your travel diary of such places and the names of contacts, for the next time you visit.

Your travel guide, local directories and the all encompassing *Yellow Pages* will supply a great range of dining choices. All that's required is some research by phone, and discussion with locals such as your concierge, beauty parlour operator or taxi driver.

STRANGE FOODS

For visitors from afar, the discovery of unique foods is an essential aspect of true adventure. Fresh local fruits tend to symbolise each area, from the start. Fine hotels welcome you with a basket of their best in your room. Northerners rarely see mangosteens with their delicate white puffs, lychees or rambutans – fresh, not out of a can. A mango or a papaya, ripe from the tree, is a rare treat when unfamiliar. Southern Asians visiting the United States have delights in store for them in the superb apples and cherries from Washington State, and shoofly pie from Louisiana.

Knife, fork and spoon are available everywhere, but sometimes local methods are fun to try. Chopsticks, for the initiated, provide a delicate, morsel-enjoying system of eating from a bowl. In India, one can learn to eat with the fingers aided with a bread called *naan* (but be careful to use your right hand, so as not to offend a host). Fried rice, with a different name in each country, is served in infinite variety – and is sometimes eaten with a large.spoon.

Southern Chinese and Southeast Asians use chillies with abandon, to enhance the taste of bland foods, thereby burning the mouths of unwary visitors. Experienced travellers learn to ask the degree of enhancement on a scale of "One, two or three chilli-hot?". A temporising waiter's reply, "Very mild," is to be treated with suspicion. In the Chinese province of Sichuan, we soon gathered that the degrees started with very hot, and accelerated to higher magnitudes. We learned preventive tactics, such as washing the morsel in clear soup, unobtrusively, before chewing.

There are eel and squid lovers, as against those of us who are not fond of the slippery and the chewy. The problem is to identify the objects by their local names – when everything is covered with sauces (and names are equally obscure) – unless you speak the language or can have them pointed out in your dictionary. In Italy they call the round, white, edible rubber bands *calamari*.

Various sizes of the other universal seafood are shrimp, prawn and tiger prawn. When these delicacies are served with their shells on, under a hot red sauce, you have to learn a new dimension of eating. The system is to spit out the inedible, indelicate though some might think it. When a whole crab is served so, who could possibly figure out how to pick apart the luscious meat without getting sprayed from chin to lap with chilli-red goo? (So one rolls up one's sleeves, tucks a napkin where it is needed, and sets to.)

☛ Personal Experience

One rare incident, I must share with you. We were dining in a cell-block-like restaurant in a hotel on the Mekong River, at Xishuang Bana, Yunnan. The rice and steamed vegetables were delightful, and side-dish saucers of crunchy titbits were served as requested. Interesting, with a garlic flavour – until we asked what the strange fried whatevers were. "Fried bees," answered our youthful guide, who condescended to finish the lot, with gusto, as we shied off.

Snake restaurants are well known in China; in Japan, poison fish (with a 99% guarantee that the poison has been removed). Vegetarian dishes conjured to look and taste like meat and fish dishes, once the domain of religious sects, are now common. A health restaurant recently opened in Manila, announcing a proper proportion of negative ions in the air to allow all believers in unadulterated and organic growth foods to dine in purity. The Japanese eat their fish raw, tempered with that strong green mustard paste *(wasabi)* in soy sauce; and some of the noodles, like some pasta, are Nile green.

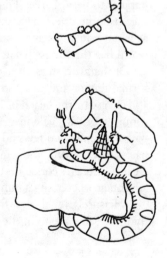

Different names for the same food can be confusing, as in 'papaya' and 'paw paw'.

Australian restaurants in various areas offer buffalo steak or kangaroo, emu and crocodile meat, as alternatives to their ubiquitous barramundi fish fillets. For first-time thrills and something to tell your children about, try some of these. Korean restaurants feature dog meat, something the rest of us (pet lovers or pet haters) have been unable even to think about.

TENDER STOMACHS

For tender stomachs or reluctant palates, we have a few basic recommendations. Ask for vegetables steamed; sauces served on the side, when in doubt; grilled meat, fish and poultry. The char from the flames is less harmful than gooey unknown sauces; besides, the chef can't hide anything that way. Admit readily to finding a taste obnoxious, as in fishy-prawn, and turn it away. Most restaurants will gladly serve something else if you ask.

A major problem arises when you sense that the person serving you doesn't understand your language too well. He will agree to everything you say, and when you get your dinner it will be all wrong. Speak up, don't be shy. Ask for the dining-room manager, compliment him on the wonderful restaurant and request that he or she personally take your order to avoid confusion. My wife hates oil and continually spends time asking for "steam cooked, no oil please". It may sound simple, but we have been surprised by the number of Eastern chefs who find themselves psychologically unable to omit oil completely.

Above all, eating abroad is an adventure: the tastes of new foods and preparation styles are treasures to be garnered. If you happen to be in Lhasa Tibet for the one and only time in your life, taste the offerings anyway. At best you will enjoy them, and at worst you will have a story to tell about how the top of the world has the lowest palatability on earth.

On lengthy stays in a particular location, we often bypass formal dinner and carry something to the room. Lunch is fruit and cheese by the beach or in the comfort of our open-windowed room or private balcony. Most hotels supply, free, the wherewithal to make coffee and tea. Breakfast can be a continental pastry or croissant, and a mango, bought the night before to eat with your tea or coffee on the veranda. A light breakfast has the advantage of creating a hunger for lunch at a friendly street cafe.

A leisurely lunch in a fine restaurant is much less expensive than the same menu in the evening. Most business lunchers eat quickly, leaving the dining room and service to you. Another advantage of eating a siesta-lunch is physical comfort. A heavy meal before you go to bed at night is uncomfortable and un-healthy. A late lunch affords time to walk it off and maybe nap before dinner, when a light meal suffices. It is difficult to get evening reservations at famous restaurants during a short city visit. The concierge will find it much easier to make a luncheon booking for you.

Snacks before retiring can easily be kept in the small refrig-erators that the better hotels provide today. If you don't like the mini-bar prices, stop at a local market and pick up your diet cola and local beer. On longer stays, we request that they take the contents of the mini-bar out to leave room for the fruit and snacks we like to keep handy. Don't be timorous. If they ignore the request, take out the non-perishables and put them nearby. When you are travelling for six weeks, you may not want 126 restaurant breakfasts, lunches and dinners in a row. Saving US$25 a day for six weeks nets over $1,000 – enough to stretch your trip for another week.

☞ **Travel Tip**
When checking into the hotel, the porter will fuss over getting you settled. At that time, we ask for our usual specials: extra pillows, removal of mini-bar, 'decaf' coffee, daily newspaper, an empty carton to ship home luggage and shopping extras, and turn off the air-conditioning please. A helpful porter, knowing how to please you, will receive a tip then and probably earn a well-deserved gratuity when you leave; meanwhile you will have all the little extra comforts and attention.

BUFFETS

Treat all buffets, *smorgåsbord* and other hyped spreads with great suspicion. Suspicion as to over-pricing, and steam-table dull-ness. Take the time and trouble to review the spread with the same discrimination as you give to a printed menu. Walk through it and mentally select the dishes that are tempting. Then consult the menu to see which of the two styles is to be the choice of the evening. The opportunity to over-eat at a buffet is there, but the stomach can absorb only so much without severe discomfort – a travel danger which it is very important to avoid.

On the positive side, well designed buffets offer the chance to try small amounts of a variety of local or other superb dishes – and to come back for a little more of what was best. There are often rare delicacies mixed in with row on row of ordinary stuff. Wafer-thin Nova Scotia salmon or Italian *prosciutto*, for instance, may be on the starter table. A resort hotel in the Philippines served a grilled dinner of prawns (two) for P350 with vegetables and rice. A barbecue buffet the next night offered unlimited supplies of the skewered prawns along with fish, chicken, meat, a variety of salads, dessert and coffee for P495. We gorged on the delicious prawns and the grill chef was only too happy to pile our plates.

True gourmet buffet *aficionados* (I consider myself one) will attack interesting buffets with a small plate, and eat in courses, carefully selecting only the finest delicacies, rarest cheeses, tenderest shrimps – and a generous slice from the leg of lamb. Side dishes are chosen for the greenest of pea pods, and hearts of the celery and artichoke. Eat each course slowly; refresh with suitable pauses between courses for conversation, palate-cleansing and perhaps the inexpensive house wine served by the glass. It takes determination and time to enjoy the feast. No one must rush you to go round the table, or look at you with disdain (don't look askance at her plate-piling, either). The culmination is to leave room for at least a thin slice of the tastiest cheesecake and the triple chocolate *Sacher Torte*. Of course, if you are in Vienna, stop at the Sacher Hotel and lunch on their famous *Torte* and chocolate-sprinkled espresso coffee.

Request your tea in a pot: "With the best Orange Pekoe if you please." Pouring from a glass serving pot on a nearby warmer is not for gourmets like yourselves. Coffee drinkers can dawdle for an hour over a favoured espresso, or an Irish coffee.

Now that's how I like a buffet, and I will pay the price if it looks that good. This is part of the system called 'Deluxe Economy'. Get your money's worth in interesting food and good service when you find them.

In summary: food can be shocking, exciting, familiar, enjoyable or distasteful – and sometimes the cause of stomach problems. Look on the bright side. It is Adventure, part and parcel of going to a new country and exploring its character – while adding to your own...

This is no time to be shy or conservative; you may never get another chance to eat fried bees or dine in a negative-ion ambience.

Chapter Thirteen

GOOD HEALTH

It sometimes comes as a shock that other countries besides yours have adequate medical facilities and medicines. Unless you're travelling in a canoe far up the Orinoco, most places in which you will travel are well equipped to handle the usual cold, sniffle and digestion ailments. Broken limbs, heart attacks and more serious problems are frightening; but they do happen, and are efficiently attended to (see Chapter Fourteen).

My doctor in Arizona complained that all his patients came back from China with some respiratory problem. Mostly true, for he handled elderly people who normally took short tours. Beijing is a large air-polluted city. Tourists rise early to get on the bus to climb the Great Wall. If the day is rainy, and there are thousands of locals and visitors around them, then on or off the bus they will have been exposed by the end of the day to every viral element in the world that induces respiratory ailments. Much the same applies in London, Jakarta, New Delhi, Athens, Los Angeles and New York – for example.

COMMON SENSE

The solution is common sense, of course. Even if you're on a scheduled tour, you can opt out and see some sights independently. Hire a taxi or private car, carry a thermos of boiled water or hot tea, and go on a weekday when the locals thin out somewhat. If susceptible to colds and viral infections, wear a nose and mouth mask and don't mind any snide remarks or pointed fingers.

When down with a cold, do the same as you would at home. Rest, aspirin, vitamin C, hot bowls of noodle soup, thermos after thermos of tea, liberally dosed with honey and lemon; and sweat it out. If it hangs on longer, see the local doctor. All hotels have access to medical assistance, many with in-house clinics. You will not be the first tourist to catch a cold in Los Angeles or Kuala Lumpur.

We older folk have misfortunes that at home would be routine. My wife had her dental bridge repaired in Beijing; I've had kidney stone problems in Chiang Mai, north Thailand. Something in the water bit my ankle at Damai Beach in Sarawak. The hotel nurse appeared immediately and applied that rare medicine called vinegar to the wounded place; this allowed me to survive to record the event.

☛ **Family Experience**
Our son-in-law, assigned to a technical project on a joint-venture mission in Beijing, fell while playing badminton. The upper leg was broken into many pieces. Unable to find a flight out for him, a local orthopaedic surgeon did the

repair surgery in an antiquated hospital, fixing the broken pieces to a metal implant. American doctors gave due credit to the surgeon when removing the metal, months later. The patient has no limp or other after-effect. The surgeon was next seen on his way to Florida to address the University Medical School on manipulating bones back into place without surgery, in the ancient Chinese way. We gratefully conclude that, though his primary skill is indeed in traditional Chinese medicine, he was good enough at Western methods to do more than get by in an inadequate hospital.

Carry a sufficient supply of your special medications and a current medical report, if you have physical problems. Most foreign doctors are professionally educated in worldwide methods and systems. It is easy and usual to telephone or fax your home doctor, for consultation in more serious or complex cases. For evacuation, most airlines have stretcher facilities – but they are costly.

By way of milder remedies, we carry Tylenol or Panadol for the usual headaches and colds, Lomotil for diarrhoea; and not much else except elimination pills in case odd foods get our plumbing stopped up. My medi-pack contains band-aids, a thermometer, corn pads, Neosporin for scratches, and lozenges.

Inoculations

Your local government health services are well acquainted with disease problems around the world. Call and ask about the area you are travelling to. For example, the Solomon Islands perennially pose a serious malaria threat. Older nemeses like smallpox, measles and typhoid sometimes recur because the world tends to forget about them. The current worry is far more serious: AIDS.

We take routine gamma globulin (good for three months) before we leave, in case we run into bad drinking water or a new hepatitis area. The theory is that a preventive shot in the butt is worth two cure-alls in the arm.

TROPICAL AILMENTS

People unaccustomed to travelling in the tropics are shocked to discover crotch and foot infections, aggravated by lack of treatment. Insect-bite contamination is often spread by scratching. Careless sunburn can be very painful. Cuts and scrapes from live coral take many days to subside, even when treated promptly. Various types of jellyfish have stingers, some poisonous enough to kill small children. Sea snakes are rarer, but more dangerous.

As always, a gram of prevention is worth a kilo of cure. Simple precautions and wise daily adventure choices go a long way to preserve good health. In humid areas, keep the skin as dry as possible with thorough towelling. Armpit, crotch, between toes, folds of skin, under breast and waist – in both men and women these parts are most susceptible to infection. At the first sign of soreness, apply medicated powders or creams. Get local medical attention immediately if it persists.

These infections spread rapidly, and soaping in the bath is the worst thing you can do. The lye content of most soaps irritates the areas further. Oil-based soaps are better. Medicated powders, such as Johnson's, are sold all over the world.

Insect Protection

The tropics are residential areas for bugs. Mosquitoes, sandflies, gnats, water mites and a million others are out to get you if you don't watch out. Certain people attract them more than others, a rapport that makes you a delicacy to the pesky creatures. Regular travellers have favourite preventives. One expert claims that the Avon product Skin-so-Soft works wonders. Jungle experts use a concoction called Autan Stick. Ask the assistant in the hotel's small-items shop for an appropriate product.

The main ingredient in repellents is diethyl toluamide (DEET). We use an Aerogarde spray and/or cream (yellow container) or Rid cream (maroon container), available in most sophisticated areas in Asia. Creams stick to the skin longer, and so are especially useful on treks, or for sitting on the beach where there may be fearsome sandflies. Apply to exposed areas of ankles, wrists and neck before you venture out. Aerosols are used less, because of their ecological disadvantages. However, they are practical for spraying clothes around those three skin areas, and as a quick refresher when flying creatures become especially irritating. Sandflies and gnats are active in the day; the mosquitoes start flying with the bats at dusk. Before eating alfresco in the evening, coat exposed areas of the ankles and neck well. Food attracts the bugs, too.

When available, use a mosquito-net at night. Even if they fend off just one irksome bug it will be worth it. Many hotels have electrically heated slow-burning, fume-dispensing tablets that kill insects. The green serpentine mosquito coils, which also burn all night, are effective if you can stand the pungent smell. Electronic sound mechanisms are reported to be ineffectual.

Ants are common in all resort areas. Ask the hotel to provide an insect spray for use while you are in residence. Keep all semblances of food in the mini-bar refrigerator out of reach.

Don't get flustered by an occasional cockroach; though nasty looking, they are not particularly dangerous to temporary visitors. But if hunting appeals to you, each cockroach killed without poison will be a small, clean blow in the world's campaign of retaliation against this ancient pest. The tropics have lots of relatives of Leroi the Lizard hanging around as local bug catchers. Thank them for their services when they appear, usually on brief forays from behind pictures or curtains.

Keep in mind that sprays are chemical and can cause skin reactions in people with allergies. Always point the spray away from the eyes and food. Creams on the forehead and near the eyes tend to mix with perspiration and spoil the vision. Use a light hat to cover that area, and put cream below eye level only. Spray the hat rim and it will keep the less persistent buzzers away from the eyes.

What to Wear

Shoes that make your feet sweat, and tight underwear abrading infected areas, are further sources of aggravation. It is better to wear substantial open sandals, like the German Birkenstocks, than sports shoes.

Loose-fitting underwear is more comfortable, as tight garments tend to rub when you walk in humid areas or adjust your position in an aeroplane seat for eight hours.

Spending a full day on the beach? Take an extra swimsuit and change the wet one under a towel so that you won't be chafing. A little practice makes expert changers of us all. Nature-lovers should take advantage of the nudist beaches to be found in many places. It's amazing how fresh air and saltwater, applied to all the nooks and crannies of the body, make them healthier. If you are shy, wear the minimum amount of textile. In either case, apply liberal amounts of sun screen, #15 at the least.

SUNBURN

Sun-induced skin cancer is almost as well publicised as lung cancer. Some doctors advise us to stay out of the sun altogether, or to wear protective hats and clothing. Unfortunately most of us are attuned to a 'tan is healthy' outlook, and we like the bronzing of our skin.

Here are two methods of enjoying the sun without overmuch risk (neither is a medical opinion). One is to use sun screen lotions, at a level no lower than 15. As to the different types, thicker creams stick longer, while watery types and sprays are seldom effective throughout a long day at the beach. Most important, never bask directly in the sun for long stretches of time. Under a palm tree or in a cabana is best. Believe me, you'll tan just as well under filtered sun as in the direct light, while avoiding the lobster-red burn which will soon peel off. Reflected sun, as in a boat on a long day's fishing, is more severe than you imagine. Wear loose shirts and sun hats. Snorkelling exposes the back to direct and reflected sun; therefore wear a tee shirt. Cloudy days simply mean the sun is filtering through, so don't disregard the preventives just because clouds are overhead.

You would think, and are probably saying, that everyone knows all this. Next time you're on the beach, look around. Pale white skins are stretched out in full array, and by dinner that night will be bright red. Remind yourself that physical comfort is the principal way to have an enjoyable vacation. For some, part of 'getting away from routine' is sexual freedom with travelling companions. Severe burns and itchy skin are definitely inhibiting.

MASSAGE AND HEALTH CLUBS

Frequent travellers indulge in body treatments for relaxation, easing of tired muscles and general physical enjoyment. Many hotels have courtesy health clubs where you can begin or continue your aerobics on a planned routine. Depending on your age and physical condition, you should only use the machinery so variously available under professional guidance. A few minutes on a bicycle won't hurt anyone – but if it isn't a sustained programme it won't help much either.

Jacuzzi and sauna are very relaxing if used in moderation. Recommendations for their use are always displayed, and the club attendants will advise you. For those who haven't dipped a toe into these luxuries, a travelling holiday makes a good opportunity to begin. Don't be shy or bashful. Enquire directly at a club, as a novice, for information and assistance. It will become a wonderful way to spend an hour or two during an exhausting tour or extended journey.

Therapeutic massage is a body toner for people not averse to stripping and letting a masseur or masseuse rub down the joints and grind out a knot behind the shoulders. There are various styles, categorised under Sports, Correctional, Relaxation, Chinese, Swedish, Japanese and so on. If you are a first-timer, don't worry; just tell the operator what you want to accomplish. Relax and have your back and buns rubbed down; and your legs, aching from all that mountain climbing. For the most part, therapists advertising publicly are competent – in varying degrees. Some little time after the first session, you will know whether they have helped you or not.

Sensual Massage

A sensual massage is another service altogether. In today's world both male and female customers are solicited – and should be guided by local laws and mores. The worldwide AIDS epidemic has instilled a tremendous amount of caution into the sexual part of the trade, via the operators. Many levels of service are offered by advertisements of 'Full Body Massage'. Operators may be clothed or partly or completely nude, depending on the local customs.

Amongst enlightened customers, eroticism can be a pleasant experience in a clean and welcoming ambience. For others, who wish to maintain the privacy of their bodies, there is no problem. Tell the operators exactly what your limitations are and they will inform you of theirs.

Escorts, male and female, and brothels, male and female, belong to the realm of prostitution. Their customers indulge at their own pleasure and risk. Enough said.

HEALTHY DO'S AND DON'TS

The items on this list are well known as common sense. Put them into practice, for more fun and happiness in your travels:

- On long flights, drink lots of liquid but little alcohol.
- Rest when you're tired.
- Take vitamin C plus an apple a day.
- In remote places, drink only boiled water.
- Avoid street snacks.
- Take a hot shower or bath after a wet or cold adventure.

- Dress for your destination.
- Whether climbing a mountain or wrestling with heavy luggage: don't exert yourself beyond your capacity.
- Wear comfortable broken-in shoes to prevent foot sores.
- Keep toes and feet dry and well aired.
- Wear loose undergarments to prevent chafing.
- Exercise daily – stretch, walk, swim or something.

Good health and the ability to cope with emergencies make travelling more adventurous and more enjoyable.

Chapter Fourteen

WHEN THINGS GO WRONG

Life does have its comeuppances. Statistics say that more accidents occur at or near home than anywhere else. I believe it, because people are most often at or near their homes. But there is always the possibility of you becoming a minority statistic by having a serious problem while travelling. Aircraft, ships, trains and road vehicles can crash. You can fall and dislocate an elbow (it happened to me in Mexico). In the Andes, far above the highest mosquito, you can be struck down by an allergy to the malaria pills you were prescribed for the rest of your Venezuelan holiday. Or, when the ticker elects to go on leave temporarily, you could be in the middle of the Sahara.

In another vein of 'it could only happen to me', passport, credit cards, cash or valuables can be lost or stolen; pre-booked and confirmed hotel reservations can be non-existent on arrival at 2:00 a.m. in a foreign country; a guide may fail to show up in time to get you to the airport for the next leg of the journey.

The essence of this chapter will be to list possible problems and probable solutions, given the likely times and places of an occurrence. The odds against the really serious things happening are equivalent to winning $10 million in a lottery. But someone always does win and, while there is a first time for any problem, you can be fairly sure that the solution to yours has already been found.

In the following discussion we assume there is a victim, and a travelling companion or nearby friend to assist.

DEATH, HEART AND ACCIDENTS

☞ **Death of a travel companion**
Seek out the nearest available embassy or consular official of your country for assistance and advice.

The most serious thing that can happen to you while you are away is to have your travelling companion die. Distress and confusion are compounded by the fact of being in a foreign country. Whether accidental or health-related, the result is the same. Local officials are equipped to handle the emergency. Cause of death will be determined, a certificate issued and your ambassador or consul will be officially notified.

Then the paperwork starts. The country will have its regulations, within which you will have to decide between cremation and repatriation for burial. Fortunately there is great empathy for persons in this saddened state. The hotel you are staying at, the travel agency handling your journey, airlines, consular officials: all will help you find the best way through the two countries' laws and procedures. Matters will be arranged with surprisingly little delay.

Obtain a proper death certificate before you go home. An official from your consulate or embassy must sign as registrar or notary. This formal document will be required in connection with insurance and administration of the estate, and for announcement of the death in a newspaper.

Hospitals and Treatment

For serious bodily injury, heart attack or dangerous illness requiring treatment in hospital, you will need evidence of a travel insurance policy and/or your credit card to show how the costs will be met.

Emergency services will get the patient to a hospital for immediate trauma care. From then on:

- Hospitals and medical personnel worry about how the emergency service and follow-up care are to be paid for. Patient and companion are concerned with survival and remedial care. Diplomatic and consular officials are not authorised to spend embassy funds for this purpose.
- An internationally recognised credit card will overcome any hospital admission problem. Proof of insurance cover will normally suffice thereafter.
- If the patient is in no state to be transported home, the major dilemma does not yet arise; similarly if the treatment available (and affordable) where you are is as good as, or better than, that in your own country. You may have instead the questions of: which local hospital; whether the companion (now hospital visitor) should move to somewhere more convenient or cheaper; and how much recovering to do before going home. (This last could be influenced by your insurer's willingness to accept a medical recommendation in favour of comfort and care in a first-class flight.) You will have to depend on local advice and your own good judgement.

Returning home as a stretcher-patient is an expensive and difficult undertaking unless you are wealthy enough to charter a flight. Most airlines use a row of seats to accommodate a stretcher, but instant booking may be difficult as transoceanic flights are often full. If there is a choice, it is far better to wait until the patient is mobile. Wheelchairs and fork-lifts are common equipment at airports.

To ease your mind, most of the world you will travel in has adequate to fine emergency care, once you have crossed the money line. Hospitals in some countries are not up to modern standards, but emergency heart care will be given until the patient can return home.

Travellers should be well aware of their potential heart or other weaknesses. Such conditions have to be taken into consideration when making travel plans. Broken limbs (which are unforeseeable) present relatively routine repair problems; initial treatment can be improved on later if necessary.

An enigma of modern travel is that the USA, with perhaps the finest health care in the world, can be the worst place in the world in which to fall seriously ill. If, for instance, you break a leg in New York and appear impoverished and without adequate insurance, the ambulance will take you to Bellevue Public Hospital where you will probably be in a queue of 50 or more people awaiting emergency treatment. However, with evidence of guaranteed payment, you would be taken to Cornell University Hospital, one of the world's finest trauma centres. Treatment can cost thousands of dollars a day in America.

Colds, Diarrhoea or General Aches and Pains
Visit local doctors or resort to common remedies. (See Chapter Thirteen.)

LOSS OF PASSPORT, CREDIT CARD OR VALUABLES
Contact your nearest consulate or embassy for passport replacement; make a detailed police report.

Valuables do get stolen, and they can be lost through carelessness. Credit card companies should be notified of card losses as soon as possible. They give certain numbers to be called in the originating country, but any local office of the credit card company will accept a lost card report. A detailed list of cards should be left at home, with the proper number to be notified by someone there as a backup. Card companies have provision for covering fraudulent charges and will not penalise you for other people's misuse of your card. Whether or not you find the card, once its loss is reported it cannot be used again. Though it is convenient for spouses to have cards with the same number, it can be maddening to be denied use of the one that is not lost. You probably won't receive a new pair of cards until you reach home. Couples who travel often should ask for separate numbers/accounts before replacements are due.

Traveller's cheques come complete with instructions for security. Your homeowner's and personal insurance policies cover you for loss of valuables. Report at once to the issuing authority the loss of such documents as air or railway tickets or personal cheques. There is always a chance that your quick reaction will result in apprehension of the thief. Fax is the best method of communication in all these instances, as it provides a quick, written and dated record of your report. But you should send on the hard copy.

Any loss claim on your insurance company must be substantiated by a verified copy of your report to the police.

LOSS OF LUGGAGE

If the loss occurs at an airport or station, report to a lost luggage authority *before you leave the building*.

Independent Travellers are aware of lost luggage as soon as the carousel stops bringing in the load and theirs has not appeared. Lost-luggage counters are nearby with forms to fill in and describe the items. Statistics show 90% recovery within 48 hours, and a further 9% later. International airlines provide small sums (US$200 normally) in cash, to get you through the night.

In the event of permanent loss, airline insurance usually limits claims to US$500 per traveller. This is detailed on your ticket and may vary between airlines. Other compensation must come from personal insurance cover.

Luggage loss when travelling with a tour group presents another problem because the tour staff will be handling your luggage. Even though they agree to collect all the bags (with tour identification tags) for your group, it's safer if you see yours come in and put with the group's pile – or at least verify that the tags are visible. Problems arise when you check in at the hotel and find out then that a case is missing. Frantic backtracking is frustrating and time consuming. If a tag has come off in the handling, the forlorn case sits on the carousel going round and round looking for its owner.

It's fun to shop, but replacing all the favourite items of clothing and nicknacks, plus inspired purchases, is an infuriating subtraction of time from the remains of the holiday. Your vacation will be remembered as the time you lost trying to replicate all your belongings. See Chapter Fifteen on keeping valuables in your hand-baggage.

☛ Personal Experience
Our last luggage loss was at Broome in Australia, where we received our cases in good order from the baggage section and then gave them to the hotel's transfer bus. One duffel was missing when we got to our room. It was late at night; the hotel porter had to find out where the bus driver had parked in town, raid the luggage compartment to find the missing bag, and return that to us two hours later. Don't wait until the next day; insist they follow up immediately.

AIRLINE BUMPING AND DISHONOURED RESERVATIONS

Demand instant satisfaction; don't leave the counter until you have it.
Some travellers are guilty of not showing up for confirmed reservations. The airlines are guilty of overbooking.

These two facts of travel commerce are the root cause, on the rare occasions when genuine passengers are turned away. The immediate cause is that this flight did not produce its quota of 'no-shows'. Getting bumped is especially disconcerting at the beginning of an extensive travel itinerary. The shock waves can cause innumerable changes down the list of reservations on your schedule.

To avoid being a victim, always show up very early for overseas flights. Early arrivals have their boarding passes in hand before anyone knows about no-shows. It is the latecomers who are bumped. If you are refused a passage despite a confirmed reservation, remain at the counter until you are satisfied with arrangements to pacify you. This could be a seat on the next available flight or on another airline flying to the same destination, whichever is the earlier. In addition the airline should offer you monetary or travel-credit compensation, all spelled out in their regulations. Overnight lodging and meal vouchers are issued on the spot for the nearest hotel if there is a next day connection.

If you show sufficient determination, and such space is available, they will upgrade an Economy seat to Business or First Class as their simplest and cheapest solution. You may suddenly find yourself holding a boarding pass for a low seat number compartment without being told. Just get on board and enjoy the extra specials. The more informal your dress, as viewed across the check-in counter, the less likely this privilege.

When You Bump the Airline
Travellers, also, can make mistakes. Our daughter's family was

once embarrassed to arrive at the airport with tickets for the previous day, confused by a 12:10 a.m. departure. They thought it was Saturday night they were leaving. Actually it was 12:10 a.m. Saturday, meaning Friday night. After the immediate chaos, passages were available that night and the airline graciously agreed to advise the destination hotel of the confusion and late arrival of their guest. It happens.

FLIGHT DELAYS AND CANCELLATIONS

Cancelled or delayed flights are the airline's problem. Staff will make alternative arrangements to the best of their ability. Be patient, but try using your own initiative to find another airline or means of transport.

Weather is the principal cause of last-minute delays and cancelled flights. A snowstorm comes in just as the plane is about to leave for a sunny climate. (Riots or local disturbances, such as the Los Angeles troubles in May 1992, can cause consternation, but usually have no effect on international flights.)

The airport is chaotic, airline personnel are frantically trying to post bulletins and pacify everyone. You are frustrated, facing disruption of your plans and, until you leave, little prospect of revising them. Severe weather may impound you in the airport, unable to return home or get to a hotel for the night. There is nothing to do but make the best of it and hope to find a comfortable seat, or a table in the restaurant, for the duration.

A delayed flight because of technical problems is a different story. You are free of your ticket obligation and may seek another airline going to the same destination. Your original airline may offer to help you – or attempt to keep you 'on line'. Try to determine how long the delay is expected to last. Minor repairs are usually complete within an hour or two. Defects requiring a replacement aircraft will keep you longer: spare planes are rarely sitting around. The airport concourse flight board will tell you of other aircraft going to or near your destination.

Before the crowd gets the word, go directly to a possible substitute airline's check-in desk and request a transfer to their flight. In most cases they know the situation and will accept your ticket if space is available. The next problem is the luggage. Your original airline must be advised of the new arrangements, to get your cases out of the bin and transfer them to the new airline. This takes time and you will be warned that it may not be possible before departure. Another problem to be faced is security. Some authorities require all luggage to be accompanied by a passenger. Switching carriers is complicated. Decisions, decisions…

Properly tagged luggage, with you in the possession of the claim checks (stapled to your ticket at check-in), will eventually get to you; it does 99 times out of 100. With domestic flying we will accept that risk and jump on the new flight. In overseas flight situations we will back out and await the arrangements of the original airline, even if it means staying overnight. Insist that the airline fax to your next hotel news of the delay, giving you a copy of the fax (or telex). Remember, you have guaranteed or prepaid the first night. Hotels recognise this travel hazard and will adjust if notified properly.

FAILED HOTEL RESERVATIONS

Stand your ground, wave your confirmation advice and demand your rights. Hotel staff are ordinary people and computers sometimes lose information through mistakes of the operators. You arrive in the middle of the night to find the hotel fully booked and your reservation, specifically marked 'late arrival, payment guaranteed', missing from the computer. It is rarely that a hotel cannot scrape up one more room, probably an upgrade suite, until they can match your reservation.

If they can offer only the couch in the lobby, they will try to shift you to another hotel, nearby if possible, and throw in a free breakfast or dinner as appeasement.

Alas you and your companion are weary from the long day's travel; it may be 24 hours since you were in bed. Disgruntled, angry and out of sorts, you can erupt with a cyclone of invective, threaten legal action and swear "never to stay at a Hilton Hotel again, as long as we live." On the other hand, you could think it through creatively and make a deal on the spot. Request some real favours like free rooms and meals or a half-price rate for the duration of your visit. There is always a duty manager on hand, who rules absolutely and can sanction virtually anything to appease you – such as complimentary rooms for your stay, a champagne dinner the next night, and maybe take care of your laundry for a week. Think about that before you give yourself a heart attack by screaming at the desk clerk.

When confronted by an absolute error on the part of an airline or hotel, discretion is the better part of valour. Make a deal: get something tangible for the discomfort you agree to grin and bear. And then be gratefully impressed by such skill in extricating you and the hotel from the unfortunate difficulty.

EMERGENCY, RETURN HOME

If serious illness (say) occurs at home and you have to go back immediately, transport is the first problem. Your travel guides will help if you are on a tour. Hotel concierges are wonderful in emergencies.

Often all you have to do is call the airline, explain the problem and request the earliest available flight. You may have to buy a new flight ticket or fly with a different company. Later, return your unused portion of the old one, for a refund, to the issuing office or travel agent. No problem.

Death or emergency in the family is the most common reason. If a new ticket is required, they will ask details to confirm the emergency and then help with a reduced fare and quick flight confirmation. On a fully-booked aircraft, you will have the first available wait-list seats, which is tantamount to confirmation.

See that the originating airline makes connecting reservations to your home city if you need this service. Thenceforward you are noted as a special passenger who requires assistance. Assigned airline personnel will see that you disembark first, and rush you to the connection. They expect you to be anxious and confused, needing assistance. If this assistance isn't offered, ask for it immediately.

Getting from a remote resort area to the main embarkation point can be more trying, depending on the time of the day, weather problems and boat or intermediate flight availability. Have faith, pack your gear – and don't forget to empty the hotel safe of your valuables. Emergencies compound frustrations into carelessness, chaos and further problems. If things go only semi-smoothly, you will be surprised how much of the globe you can traverse in less than a day.

After the crisis, return tickets or vouchers for all unused parts of prepaid travel to your booking agent, or direct to the carrier if booked that way, along with a complete statement of the emergency. Partial or full refunds will be forthcoming.

RIOT, HIJACKING AND POLITICAL DISTURBANCE

If unrest looks likely before you leave, cancel and go somewhere else. If trapped, keep cool and make the best of the situation.

We never go to an area or country where there is actual or expected trouble. We are not attracted to the 1994 Middle East, the less stable of the former Iron Curtain countries, or much of Africa. Riot-torn areas of New York, Los Angeles or cities in other lands do not appeal to us. There are hundreds of pleasant, peaceful, relaxing and very interesting areas to visit without endangering ourselves or spoiling the fun and adventure of travelling. For instance you can fly into Los Angeles Airport, and immediately fly out to safer and more interesting parts of the continent. North are San Francisco, Colorado and Canada. East

are Arizona, Louisiana and the Midwest. South are Mexico and the resorts of Baja California. In Thailand, the same advice leads you to avoid Bangkok. Fly north to Chiang Mai, south to Ko Samui and Hua Hin or west to the resorts of Phuket and Pattaya. Why waste time in the danger/discomfort areas?

When a Riot Occurs

Again, you have lottery odds against being involved in wild or serious local conflicts. The rule of thumb is to remain as cool as possible and think of the best and quickest way to get out. If hijacked, do what comes naturally: tuck your head down and pray. The police and military are equipped and trained to take the risks. If riots erupt around your area, stay in the hotel close to other foreign nationals. Rioters seldom want to harm visitors; there is no benefit in needling foreign governments. Authorities and embassy staff will automatically go all out to protect you and arrange a speedy exit. They too are trained for this.

Whatever happens, don't fret about your luggage. Stow your documents and valuables in your best shoulder bag or waist pouch, ready to leave unencumbered. If there is time, change to the most practical clothes you have. Your main concern is survival. Anything else is secondary.

PSEUDO-GUIDES AND SCAMS

Take particular care when arriving at airports, train stations, ship harbours and scenic sites independently. Many unsophisticated tourist destinations are infiltrated with pseudo-guides or hustlers anxious to latch on to travellers.

The scams are operated by offering guide services to visit, for example, the holy places of Jerusalem or the pyramids of Egypt. After a meagre tour, the unofficial guide demands an exorbitant sum for services rendered. To further intimidate the tourist who protests, loud voice and professed indignation enhance the performance.

When confronted with such a situation, insist the matter must be settled at your hotel or possibly a police station. Thus you can get arbitration assistance. In most instances, the mere threat to do that will settle the situation quickly and fairly. Ignore any aftermath curses; it's all part of the performance.

The recommended procedure is never hire instant guides on the street or in transportation arrival zones. Some countries have official information centres for tourists. In other cases, wait until you have checked into your hotel, then enquire for proper and well-known guides and tours. Heed the advice you give your children, and 'never get into a car with a strange man'.

The same category of hustler or team will offer blackmarket currency exchange with a direct intention to cheat.

In Beijing, for instance, a tourist was offered a much better exchange than the official rate on renminbi (yuan) for dollars. After agreeing to the transaction, the victim handed over his dollars for a thick stack of yuan. While he was counting, another member of the scam team appeared, dressed like an official person, with badge and armband. He demanded an explanation for the illegal transaction. The frightened victim saw the pseudo-official chase the offender away, disappearing himself in the process. The finished count of yuan was far short of even the official exchange rate.

> **Blackmarket money exchange, illegal in most countries, is fraught with problems and sometimes physical danger. It isn't worth it.**

MISADVENTURES

The following incidents happened to us during our first 25 years of foreign travel.

Cabo San Lucas, Baja California

I fell while climbing a hillside and pulled my elbow out of its socket, fainting at the immediate shock. I managed to walk the mile and a half of beach back to the hotel, and was rushed into San Jose del Cabo's small-town clinic. The X-ray was out of commission, but the nurse patched up my skin abrasions and we went nine miles to a doctor's residence in Cabo San Lucas. The pregnant wife of the doctor took the X-ray in her kitchen, and developed it in the bathroom while the doctor shot me up with a painkiller. The three of them pulled the arm back into its socket, strapped up a sling and charged me US$20. On return to the States, my doctor took another X-ray, confirmed that everything had been done properly, and charged me $125.

I recovered completely. My wife, frantic at the time, still worries it may happen again and always warns me to be careful.

Beijing

This time Eileen broke a tooth out of her bridge. We were taken to the hospital; the nice doctor (in China, as elsewhere in the East, dentists are known as doctors) marvelled at the modern contraption. She managed to re-attach the tooth with a metal screw, and charged nothing. We left 20 yuan (US$6) under the tray, and our trip went on. Our home dentist marvelled at the repair in lieu of replacement, re-did the bridge screwlessly, and charged only $150. He did say that the screw would probably have held for ever.

Bangkok

We lost our luggage in transferring overnight from Hong Kong to Singapore. We went on to Singapore, trying to make a list of everything in the three missing cases. Qantas gave us S$200 to cover emergencies. The luggage turned up two days later, delivered to us at the Shangri-La.

Malaysia

A jellyfish attack and insect bites caused severe inflammation. Both were soothed by the hotel nurse. The insect bites persisted and required antibiotics and skin treatment on returning home.

In another incident, we were en route from Kuching in Sarawak, via an aircraft switch at Kuala Lumpur, to Tioman Island. Our flight was delayed, then cancelled, in Kuching. Since all flights from KL to Tioman were fully booked, we flew to Singapore, stayed overnight and took a direct flight to the island of Tioman. Malaysian Airlines refunded our tickets with a credit voucher, but declined to pay overnight compensation.

Korea

We neglected to take passports and valuables from the hotel safe. The mistake was discovered at the airport, where one of us kept a foot (as it were) in the check-in and the other hired a taxi to return to the hotel (30 minutes away) and come back, arriving 10 minutes before flight time. Harassing, but not life-threatening.

Shanghai – 4 June, 1989

The Tiananmen Square massacre in Beijing affected all foreigners. Our problem was getting to the airport through riotous streets in Shanghai. The airport was a mass of humanity, all trying to arrange flights. Customs and immigration personnel were concerned to get the foreigners out. Our previously booked Cathay Pacific flight from Shanghai to Hong Kong took off on schedule, no problem, half full.

☛ Personal Reflection

In our quarter-century of foreign travel, we have had dental and medical assistance many times; and surgery on a cancerous node on my cheek once, in Singapore. We have been treated by hotel clinics countless times after emerging from the wilds with colds, sores, infections and a self-solving case of kidney stones. All of these while covering an estimated quarter-million miles, in some 60 months away from home. By adhering to common sense and good hygiene, we survived and enjoyed the adventures to the fullest extent of our physical and monetary limitations.

Chapter Fifteen

LUGGAGE

One of the biggest bugbears in travelling is to find yourself at a railway station in (say) Japan or China, with a double flight of steps to the tracks and no porter around to tote your luggage. Most fully-packed cases will weigh close to 20 kilos no matter what your good intentions are. Any more than 20 kilos in one bag is risking a heart attack. A couple travelling with two normal duffel bags – and an extra one with books, snacks, shoes, appliances and a supply of optical rinse for their lenses – will carry 40+ kilos.

AVOID HEART SHOCK

Talk about culture shock! Lugging 40 to 50 kilos up two flights of stairs is enough to give your heart a good shock. Now before you get all het up and vow never to go away without all of your necessities, let's get down to brass tacks about what you really need to carry. We concede you may already have luggage with built-in wheels, or a folding luggage trolley, to negotiate the airports. Larger trolleys are available to get you into and out of the concourse with little pain. Hotels do have porters (though not always, in some countries). Given all these facts, you will still have to lift the cases many times to pack, unpack and take them on and off the trolleys at security inspection stations. A month or six weeks of this can cause a lot of backaches, maybe a hernia, and especially an argument with your travelling companion on the theme "how can we need all this?" As in all health recommendations, prevention is far better than cure. It boils down to a nutshell of advice: *travel light.*

CHOOSE WISELY

It is admittedly easier and cheaper to use the same old hard case luggage you've had for years. But with your newfound love of travel we suggest you give it away and invest a modest amount in new cases. Shop carefully: there are bargains, and interesting units that have separate pockets for everything. Others come in glitzy hard plastic, with folding handles and tiny wheels guaranteed to catch on every ripple in the pavement. Some weigh three or four kilograms before you put a toothbrush in them.

We recommend soft-sided duffels, as least subject to handling damage, and with a capacity to swell, if need be, to accommodate extra items. Preferred styles have double zipper tops that can open fully. Thus you can get a tee shirt out of the bottom without having to unpack completely. Two basic requirements override all other advantages:

- *Durable material* such as canvas or a tough synthetic. Canvas is less likely to be pierced by a sharp object, and its durability is evidenced by the long-lasting love for blue jeans originated by Levi Strauss a century ago. Outside zipper compartments use up more room than they provide, with the additional danger of being ripped off. Carry-on and beach duffels on the other hand should provide many useful extra compartments.
- *Support straps* absolutely must go all round the case in one piece and extend to become the carrying handles. No other

arrangement is acceptable, regardless of what the salesperson tells you. With continued use, separately stitched handles and partial bindings will tear off sooner or later. If you don't believe me, peek behind the scenes of the luggage carousel at the airport and watch the muscle men play basketball with your case, flipping it onto the track.

Other things to look for are *removable shoulder straps* that clip on and off easily. Try them in the store before you buy. Remove the strap and tuck it inside before you check the case in at the airport.

Purchase tough *luggage tags* that can strap on securely. Print your name large and bold enough to be seen easily from 10 feet away. Use an office or family/friend's address with telephone and fax number, because you may not be at home when someone wants to tell you that your luggage has been found. Use the airline's cardboard string-tags also, to repeat your name and hotel destination.

Colours should be nondescript but easily recognisable, and the cases should match.

Have *luggage locks* with the same key. Small and efficient locks with matching keys will keep strange fingers out of your case. Moreover, lock the zipper to the ring embedded in the bag, if yours has this facility. Double zipper cases need two locks each, and a few extra in case you lose one or need another for hand luggage. They can be small and inexpensive, and we hide extra keys in a purse or carry-on bag. Our favourite key-holder is in the style of a small Swiss Army pocket knife (with scissors, blade, file, tweezers and toothpick, plus a key loop at one end) carried on the person. It's easy to get to if the customs and immigration people want you to open up.

Stolen luggage is rare; lost luggage, more common. However, 1% of a billion airline passengers per year amounts to 10 million pieces of lost or stolen luggage. Most lost luggage is found and returned within 48 hours. You don't want to be among the 1% – or even be annoyed by the loss and then return of your belongings. Platinum American Express Credit Card replicas for luggage tags are flattering, but they advertise the wealth of their owners. Flashy expensive leather cases also are tempting to an airport or hotel thief.

Tie a bright yellow ribbon on the handle to recognise your own quickly, but always check your name tag. There is a great sameness about much of today's luggage.

For two people on longer trips, we suggest one 36-inch duffel bag for each, and another smaller matching piece for combined extras such as snorkel gear, spare shoes, rain cape, etc. Usually one carry-on is sufficient for two unless you are taking camera equipment or portable computer gear: for you don't want to trust the bouncing around of valuable equipment to check-in luggage systems if you can avoid it.

Carry-on shoulder bags must be within the airline size limit and fit into the sample frame before you board the plane. All luggage stores have those dimensions available. These bags should be of light synthetic fabric, with side pockets for a book, snacks and whatevers. Inside are your cosmetics, change of clothes, and arrival sweater or a very light rain jacket. Cameras, binoculars, jewellery and other valuables are best carried therein.

Carry-ons are with you all the time, and cover immediate needs if your main luggage is lost. They should be light in weight, and have straps that go all the way round to become handles. A cardboard insert for the bottom gives a flat support for the folding trolley.

Carry at least one such small trolley to trundle the hand baggage, because many large airports have long distances to walk to and from the departure and arrival gates. Trolleys are also invaluable when shopping in town or going to the post office with extras to be shipped home. Criteria for a folding trolley are lightness, a good platform and large wheels. An elastic cord helps to hold the load tightly.

PACKING

Lay out everything you absolutely need for the trip and then leave half of it at home.

For some weird psychological reason, we travellers tend to take more clothes than we need, except when the absence will be so long that it is off our scale of reckoning. Women are alleged to be greater offenders than men. Though we have travelled for a quarter of a century, Eileen is guilty of last-minute paranoia, sneaking in that extra pair of shoes, sweater, tee shirt or whatever just as we are leaving. It is a crime punishable by a sigh and a frown from me. The next family will have these roles reversed. Efficient packing is a matter of nesting like items together, folding without wrinkles, and filling each corner with what best fits it.

159

Where are you going and what will you be doing? The first step is to review the itinerary. Begin with comfortable everyday travel garb in the ratio of one mix-and-match outfit for every three days, up to three sets. Women or men, the same. Thus if you are on a tour bus your neighbours will be amazed to find you have something different on every day for almost a month. Women like to put on the spangles or pretties for dinner at night, if not in a tent camp in the wilds of Nepal. The expected climate will modify the outfits. Except for formal dining in the larger cities, a jacket, shirt and tie at dinner is up to the man. On a cruise ship, they do dress up, and often require formal attire.

That is the basic gamut: from a tee shirt and shorts to tuxedo and long gowns. Not so easy, is it? Frame your selection almost through a day-by-day imagination of what you will be doing, and thus wearing. Believe me, most countries have a good supply of jumpers in case you run into unexpected cold or wet weather. Resorts have stacks of colourful sports wear at modest prices to augment your casual unisex beach or dining room rig. Birkenstocks and Reeboks are now sold by most of the world, in case your old shoes should suddenly deteriorate. Kodak film, Crest toothpaste, Johnson's baby powder and Coca Cola have sold worldwide for decades; there is no need for extra supplies. Tylenol and Panadol are often found on the shelf together with Fisherman's Choice and Ricola throat lozenges.

The big extras that weigh people down are duplicate clothes for an informal travel itinerary that have no possibility of being worn. If your custom is to dress every night for dinner, add a separate mix-and-match set for variety. That is, a man needs a choice of shirts but can survive with one jacket and tie; while a woman requires at least three basic outfits, to be accessorised with scarves and cardigan-style overblouses.

Speedy laundry service is available, making several changes of clothes unnecessary. You will find packets of detergent in our list of necessities; better hotels now supply them along with the body lotion and shampoo. For quick drying, rinse garments well, wring out then wrap in a towel to remove excess moisture before hanging up.

Local tee shirts and casuals are inexpensive and fun to wear. If your light slacks wear out or tear, buy another pair. Eileen gets a great kick out of picking up an inexpensive clever outfit and wearing it that night for dinner. If a cold snap of weather suddenly chills you, add an extra undershirt or two to your outfit, especially if dining *alfresco*.

☛ Personal Experience on Proper Dress

We were in the mountain country of Bhutan on a 10-day small group tour. A friend in Hong Kong suggested we call on the king's relatives in Thimbu as a courtesy to him and a great ego lift to us. Our guide proudly made the connection – the Dorgi family would gladly receive us that evening at six. Our total wardrobe was one duffel with one mix and match each. What to wear for the royal appearance? We donned our cleanest shirt and slacks, with a nylon jacket apiece, and removed the travel dust from our shoes. The royal family cordially received us in their Los Angeles-style suburban home. Three uncles, attired in slacks and tennis shoes, had just finished playing golf. The first and second wives of each uncle wore slacks and tee shirts. Our appearance at court was accepted. Unfortunately King Wangchuk was absent, out hunting tigers.

PLAN AHEAD

The standard procedure is to lay out all the possibilities of clothes, accessories and equipment, days ahead of departure. Readjust every time you pass by and look at the pile. After – long after – you have decided, select the necessary luggage.

Use the checklist enclosed or make your own for continued use every year. Would you believe that I actually forgot my camera and binoculars last year? Another trick we use is to store items only used in travel in the small suitcase on our return each year in order to remember them next time. Avoid large cases like the plague for this simple reason, a variant of Parkinson's Law: 'Travellers' luggage expands to fill the space available.' If you exceed the limits of your 36-inch duffel, take two smaller ones, not one larger one. Remember your back and the hundred times you would have to lift the damned thing during the journey.

Inveterate readers should buy paperbacks, and give them away when finished. Hotel staff, guides and other providers of extra friendly service appreciate free books that are not always available to them. In China for instance, a gift of a well-thumbed *Time* or *Newsweek* magazine is treasured. Books are doubly treasured. In tightly controlled countries this can be a problem for the recipient. We get round that by leaving the item (in a bag) where the obvious beneficiary can find or choose not to find it.

Sending a dozen books home costs more than replacing them or buying fresh ones. The 10 best-sellers are sold all over the world today and are seldom worth a permanent place on the shelf. On the other hand, books of local or special interest, bought abroad, become part of my permanent collection.

Get rid of extra weight as you accumulate new clothes or souvenirs. Shipping goods home is covered in Chapter Eighteen: postal services are the chief thread of communication between nations. Prices are relatively uniform (10 kilos sent surface/sea mail averages US$35) and it takes but a few minutes to hump a box to the post office in any city. Post offices sell boxes which they think are more suitable than yours.

CONSERVING SPACE – HINTS FOR PACKING

Women's Wear
Roll or fold each set of the mix-and-match outfits together as a single unit. Pack underwear in one silk or plastic bag.

Men's Wear

Flatten long and short trousers, then fold or roll them together as one. Flatten tees and similar heavier collared shirts, then fold or roll in the same manner. Put shirts on a single hanger, neatly; remove the hanger and fold over once. This is the last item to be packed, giving a soft and protective cover.

General Wear

- Stack shoes vertically along one end, in banded pairs.
- Fill shoes with hose and small articles.
- Make two vertical piles of the clothing pushed to each side.
- Breakables, cosmetic and medical containers, in the middle.
- Sweaters, jackets, little-used things, on the bottom.
- Robe, pyjamas, clean outfit on the top.
- Underwear, swimsuits, other crushables along sides.
- After packing stand the case on end, letting clothes compress.
- New room found at the end takes last-minute items or books.

The basic theory of packing is to fill the spaces neatly and compress the air out of folded clothes. Folds take up space and leave air corners. Rolling forces the air out and compacts the units. The mix-and-match outfits in sets allow you to take one unit out at a time. You can remain semi-packed for short stays with this system. For longer stays, especially in humid climates, unpack completely for airing. *Never use dresser drawers for short stops.* Hang or pile on chairs or shelves. Nine-tenths of left behind items were forgotten in a drawer, and the rest were on hooks in the bathroom. If you pack as suggested, following the same routine at each stop, missing items will be easily noticed.

CHECKLIST

For the record, we list a compendium of normal non-clothing requirements for a 30-day tropical adventure. We have in mind two people, staying at 4- or 5-star resorts and hotels, and using aeroplanes, trains, coastal steamers, buses and cars. Items for esoteric or special adventures are treated in specialised publications.

- Passport and insurance documents.
- Tickets and itinerary.
- Traveller's cheques and/or cash.
- Credit cards, driving licences and personal identification items.
- Address book or handheld computer with address data.
- Small pocket-size calculator, solar powered.
- Waist pouch for documents.
- Hot rod or hot pot (120-240 volts) for room coffee or tea.
- A set of electrical adaptors and an AC/DC converter.
- Your preferred coffee/tea packets.
- Vitamin C for daily intake to forestall colds.
- Capsules of odourless garlic (for those attuned).
- Lomotil, or similar diarrhoea remedy.
- Prescribed medicines in sufficient quantities for the trip.
- Thermometer and band aids.
- Favourite sunscreen.
- Small packets of detergent to wash your undies.
- Extra folding light nylon duffel to accommodate overload.
- Light plastic rain capes and an umbrella.
- Light nylon lined long jacket for change of temperature.
- Small scissors and nail files along with cosmetics.
- Ziploc bags, rubber bands and a few feet of nylon cord.
- Pocket-size binoculars and camera.
- Shaving kit and toothbrushes (electric or normal).

Hair dryers are common in hotels. If you are going to rough it, you won't need one anyway. If you forget your toothbrush or safety razor, don't fret, the aeroplane and hotel usually have spares to offer, as well as sewing kits. Cosmetics are best carried in lined soft containers. For extra protection use Ziploc bags for the leakables and seepables, inside the main bags.

Waist pouches are handy for documents and immediate cash for day tours or on beaches. The carry-on case should have cosmetics, change of clothing, reading material and snacks. A woman on her own will often use an extra large purse/handbag to avoid two units. Two people travelling together can usually get by with one carry-on between them. All important documents should be on your person for ease in filling out forms, and passing immigration and customs.

CLOTHING LISTS
These are suggested requirements for four to six weeks in the tropics.

Basics for Women:
- Three mix-and-match ensembles:
  a) Three blouses with skirts of various lengths.
  b) Three tee shirts and shorts/culottes/wraparounds.
  c) Three assorted tops and three pairs of slacks.
- Light sweater, decorated for evening wear.
- Cardigan/sweater neutral-colour ensembles for chilly evenings.
- Light nylon rain jacket, lined.
- Swimwear* plus lingerie, hose, kerchiefs.*
- Shoes: beach clogs, walking sandals (dress and casual).
- Make-up tools, not to exceed one small vanity case.
- Hats* to suit personal custom.
- Fine jewellery, but only what you wish to wear.
- Non-precious jewellery, according to taste.

* *You may do better if you buy most of these, plus sarongs and other local outfits, where you find them.*

☞ **Eileen Says:**
Use one neutral basic colour generally throughout the

collection. Then match other items to contrast or blend to taste. For instance, dress and casual shoes in the same neutral basic or blend, to avoid carrying extra pairs of different colours. A cardigan of neutral colour can be used over anything. Travel with the minimum, and have fun adding to the collection as you go. With rare exceptions, everything must be washable. Select one combination for all your air travel. Include a long-sleeved, warm shirt with an undershirt for the cold aircraft. Wear sandals or shoes that will take swollen feet, essential on long flights. Make-up, toothbrush and a spare blouse to freshen up before arrival make for a cheery landing.

Basics for Men:
- Three pairs of slacks/jeans, casual and dress.
- Three pairs of shorts, casual and dress.
- Three long-sleeved sports shirts.
- Three short-sleeved sports shirts.
- Three knit/polo tee shirts.
- One neutral-colour sports jacket.
- One neutral-colour tie.
- Sturdy sandals, trainers/walkers, dress loafers/smart slippers.
- Swimwear, underwear and socks.
- Lined rain jacket for outerwear in cool or wet weather.
- Light cotton sweater.

☞ **Fred Says:**
Everything should be washable except for the dress trousers and sports jacket. Pack non-iron clothes wherever possible: just rinse and hang out to dry. Jacket and tie are optional. Sneak in at least one outfit of well-worn clothes to knock around in on jungle or beach walks. Select your most comfortable combination for air travel. You need deep trouser pockets to prevent your wallet from falling out, and a shirt pocket that will hold your passport temporarily. Long-sleeved

shirts are recommended for the cold aircraft. Feet swell on long flights. My favourite footwear is a velcro-latched pair of Bally loafers that I can still get my feet into on arrival. Tracksuit style trousers with elastic waist – loose fitting and wrinkle resistant – reduce the discomfort of long periods in the air.

FINAL NOTE

When packing, make your own checklist in detail of exactly what you are taking. Carry it with your travel documents. It is a useful prompt when repacking – and invaluable for claiming lost luggage. On return, add items you should have taken, drop off those you shouldn't, and put the list in a safe place for the next trip. You are thus ready with your own specifications, updated after each adventure. We keep one duffel in the cupboard with travel items not used at home, so that we don't forget.

Chapter Sixteen

CAMERAS AND PHOTOGRAPHY

We all have our own ideas about taking pictures. I will not try to advise serious photographers because they know what they need. For others: *Think small.* Inexpensive 35 mm cameras abound, with flash enclosed to do all the mechanical thinking for you. A travel analysis once proved that for non-professionals, under good lighting conditions and flash, the inexpensive camera produced results almost identical to those of the finest Nikons and Leicas. Thinking cameras are more efficient than humans in adjusting for light, shadow, distance and focus.

Experience tells us that the easier the camera is to use, the more pictures you will take. Your 36-exposure rolls of 100-, 200- or 400-rated colour print film will net you 38 or 39 usable pictures. Enough to let you throw away the ordinary ones, and enlarge and show off the really good ones. Video cameras and camcorders replace what used to be the vogue for handheld movie cameras. Many of them are relatively small with complex abilities. Competition amongst the manufacturers is fierce, bringing new and interesting models continually to the market. Shop thoroughly, visiting more than one store, for the equipment that meets your needs and ability. After you decide on the model, then you can look for competitive prices.

SELECTING A CAMERA FOR THE AMATEUR

Most homes have a camera or two sitting around that have been in the family for years. Let me urge you to leave them at home and buy a new one. All television, computer, VCR, tape recording and music equipment newly on the market is far in advance of the old. Twelve months and a computer is antiquated. Televisions and VCRs are obsolete in 10 years or less. Cameras have changed radically in the past five years.

For the average non-professional user, the 35 mm cameras currently on the market do everything. They focus, adjust for light, automatically roll the film, flash lights when you can shoot, and snigger when you forget to open the lens.

Recognised brand names are in the price range of US$100 to US$250. Using an average 400-grade colour print film, you will have more than the promised 24 or 36 pictures from each roll, with never a miss.

The next step-up in proficiency is the camera with built-in telephoto and wide-angle adjustments to give longer or wider scope, but still for the average user. Clever built-in electronics date each picture; and there is an option to switch to manual adjustment. Most have timers to set for delayed action, allowing the photographer to jump into the picture. All of this is manageable by anyone interested enough to do a few tricks.

Higher levels are best left to the semi-professionals or hobbyists, who will make their own studies of the equipment on the market. They travel with multiple cameras, multiple lenses, tripods and filters, and are interested in the adventure of travel as seen through the camera lens.

If you haven't used your camera for a year or more, install new batteries whether you need to or not.

Read the instructions, whether the camera is new or old. After a few months, technical details are easily forgotten. Most pamphlets are brief and with diagrams. Long before you leave, expose a whole roll using all the systems and suggestions for use. Pretend you are abroad. Take shots in your local park, at different times of the day (and similarly at night, indoors), with an assortment of subjects. While simple cameras are literally foolproof, there is real skill in framing the scene, and judging distance, background and time of day. Doubly so for the more complex video cameras.

With video cameras, follow the same line of reasoning as above. Handheld camcorders, capturing picture and sound, are down to palm size; the larger shoulder-braced styles are outdated. Remember that they are *movie* cameras. Either the photographer or the subject being recorded has to move. It is important to decide what you are going to take before you press the start button.

There are consumer books to assist selection – necessary if you are going to become involved with the fancier 35 mm's or video camcorders. If you want to build your own library or are interested in travel lecturing, take the time to study the equipment possibilities before you buy. There is sufficient variety on the market to confuse the most knowledgeable photographer.

FILM

The most common film today is 35 mm colour print (Kodacolor, Fujicolor and the like). Actually you are taking still negatives on a strip of movie film. New printing machines process the film mechanically, and produce colour prints. Alternatively, colour-negative film is available where the end product is individually mounted slides that project a finished picture onto a screen. Black-and-white is used by professionals for newspaper and fax reproduction. The speedy develop-and-print, commonly advertised as a one-hour service, is always for 35 mm colour print. Black-and-white or colour-negative film requires laboratory processing.

Film is rated for the speed at which it reacts to light. Ratings of 1000 used by professionals will record images with a minimum amount of light, for instance incandescent bulbs in a dimly lit cave. For the average user, 100, 200 and 400 are suitable, helped by flash for indoor shots. Modern cameras are very intelligent; they interpret the rating when you insert the film. The marking 'DX' on the box indicates that the film will tell the camera what kind it is. The camera will then adjust its sensing equipment to match the right amount of light to the speed of the lens.

400 is recommended for general use inside and outside, especially for parties, people and action. It will 'stop' the motion without blurring. For example, your beloved taking off and descending in a parasail over the ocean at the end of a boat's tether. Or a friend can snap you both dancing romantically in the evening on the veranda in the bright moonlight.

100 is used for general scenery, outdoor shots in bright daylight, or reflected sun in beach and water scenes. This slower reacting film will respond with a finer grain and better detail, for instance on a day's cruise to the Great Barrier Reef for deep water fishing, snorkelling or diving. It is better for recording grand scenery shots – e.g. of the White Cliffs of Dover or the Grand Canyon.

200-speed film is the common choice when you don't know which to use. Frankly, I carry three rolls of 400 and one roll of 100 because most of our photographs are of ourselves and other people in foreign locations. We average photographers take a few shots here and a few shots there, as the mood hits us. We have sometimes left a partly exposed roll in the camera for months, awaiting an opportunity to finish it. If that is you, too, then use a 200-rating film, and you'll never know the difference. And you won't have to remember which film you have in the camera.

Serious but amateur photographers like our friend the album maker, who appears in this chapter's last paragraph, will use 24-exposure rolls of 100 and 400, shooting a whole roll in one episode or day's adventure. He installs a fresh roll especially for the day's events, with the proper rating. The only problem with this approach is money. Developing and printing 20 or 30 rolls can cost a lot, not counting the money to buy the film in the first place.

Don't fret; be yourself, shutter-bug or occasional snapper. Remember that you have brought the camera to serve your holiday purposes. Don't let photography get in the way of your fun. With some help from the pictures, your memory will hold the best record.

BASIC GUIDELINES

Never shoot into the light source; put your back to the sun.

Take a moment to frame the shot for size and suitable background. What you see in the viewfinder is what you get. The viewing lens has built-in guidelines, for you to select the parameters of the shot. The nose should be in the middle of a person's picture. A focal point, such as a tree or rock, can be the centre of a scenery shot.

Scenery and people do not mix well. The result will be too small a subject or a narrowly restricted scenic shot. If you can't see the smile clearly, you are too far from your subject. (But perhaps the scene is the point, and the person merely establishes Nature's grander scale – or proves who was there.)

When the portrait is the picture, your camera has a trick to give you the best of both. The instructions will tell you to focus on the prime subject, allowing the camera to adjust for distance, focus and lighting. Then half-depress the lens button (a light will normally show in the viewfinder), and move the camera slightly to one side to balance the person with the scene. Finish pressing the button. The result should be pleasing, as the subject is well focused; yet you can see the surf pounding in the background. *Take several shots. Film is less expensive than the cost of getting to the scene you are shooting.*

Use the flash where faces are shaded (you have to adjust the gadget on the camera sometimes). Facing a brightly lit area, such as a beach, the subject's face will be dark and unrecognisable. A turn of the face, to catch the best light on the nose and eyes, will capture the moment.

For albums take one shot of the place-name, i.e. hotel entrance, airport arrival building or resort facade. When travelling by car, stop and snap the road sign welcoming you to the area. This is a shot where person and object can share the foreground.

International Friendship

Don't be shy. Line up the camera, then ask someone nearby to press the button after you get into the scene. You need no linguistic skill. Sign language communicates what you desire.

Some people make fun of the 'typical Japanese tourist' with hanging cameras. I have found such fellow travellers especially cordial when asked by gesture to take a picture of us with our camera. I have yet to be refused and we will often take the same shot with their equipment. In this vein, when I see a couple taking pictures of each other, one at a time, I offer to snap them both. Sign language works very well and the smile of appreciation is thanks enough.

Video tapes need editing, with or without voice-overs. More than with a still camera, the tendency is to overdo each scene. If you show it all when you get home, the audience will soon fall asleep. Remember to take shots of place names and moving people and objects, to make a pleasing reminder. There is only one Steven Spielberg: the rest of us are amateurs. But you can learn something from him. Plan your shots ahead and take extra footage; then edit, edit, edit.

Final Hint

Do as the professionals do, take lots of still shots, with different angles and poses. Then – and this hurts – keep the good ones and throw away the others. One friend of ours selects only the very best, has them enlarged into 8 x 10 prints, and makes a special decorated album of each travel odyssey. They include printed memorabilia such as itineraries, menus, playbills, letters and cards from people met. It is a pleasure to look through the couple's recent and past adventures – concise and very interesting.

Chapter Seventeen

PASSPORTS, VISAS AND CUSTOMS REGULATIONS

A passport is a legal identification of citizenship used for travelling outside your country. To the uninitiated, applying for a passport sounds fearsome and complicated. Once you have done all the paperwork and have made the proper application, you are clear for a few years. Most countries issue passports for 5 or 10 years. Be patient and get the job done; then you can relax.

Government passport control offices have the application forms and will normally mail them to you for convenience. They will advise you if a personal appearance is necessary to complete and issue the document. In some countries you can collect blank forms from a post office. Current photographs (of passport size) and evidence of birth/citizenship are required. Passport pictures are easily obtained in any metropolitan area. It's not necessary to get professional portraits. The purpose of the passport picture is to allow the foreign immigration officer to compare the photo with your face to make sure the passport is yours.

Most film developing shops advertise the service. Special polaroid cameras and film are normally used, producing the result in sets of four, while you wait. Automatic photo-booths in train stations and elsewhere will do the job more cheaply but less handsomely. Get extra sets while you are about it, especially if the shop has produced an acceptable likeness; it may be cheaper by the dozen. You could need them for visas or part-time employment applications. The passport is with you for many years so when you pose for the picture, look serious; do not wear a hat – or glasses, unless you travel in them.

In many countries you will need a citizen who has known you for years to vouch that you and your photographs match the particulars in your application. The rest of the process is queuing up one morning to conclude the matter if, indeed, you have to. It's best to obtain the passport long in advance of your planned travel. Last-minute applications are often difficult, an irritation to citizen and bureaucrat alike.

VISAS

That official stamp in your passport authorising you to enter a particular country is obtained either on arrival in that country, or by application to its consulate well before you leave. Whether you need one in advance, and how to get it, can be discovered from many sources: by telephone from the local consulate or tourist office of the country you are going to visit; country-specific travel guides give details of requirements; travel agents booking your itinerary automatically provide the information.

The countries that do require a pre-issued visa need an application with current photographs attached. For nations that do not have local foreign consulates, you must apply to their nearest office. Some require you to go in person to their consulate, make the application and present your passport. Losses in registered mail (or a visa office) do not happen often; in such a case the victim has a real problem to get everything re-issued in time. Travel agents, as well as providing the information, will in some cases handle the applications when you book with them. Handing over passports to a third party is alarming even to experienced travellers. *Always get a receipt with a signature you can read.* Any unusual delay should be followed up assiduously, lest it turn into a holiday-threatening muddle. Your agent, fortunately, is motivated to rescue his reputation and your booking.

Australia and Japan (for instance) require pre-issued visas for many nationals. These authorise a specified period of years with entry entitlement for multiple visits. On a normal tourist visa China allows only one visit within a specified period – i.e. a single entry. Thus if you visit Guangzhou, and decide to go next door to Hong Kong, you have to re-apply before returning to China. Each country has its own system; it behoves you to find out exactly what is required, early in your planning.

On receiving the visa, whether pre-issued or on arrival, *read the time limits carefully* and examine the actual visa stamp before you leave the immigration counter. Thailand allows three weeks, and if you stay on the beach at Phuket a few days longer they will fine you. Malaysia can be confusing because West Malaysia issues one visa; then, if you go on to Sarawak or Sabah, you will need another visa with a different time-span. The Solomon Islands, I'm told, will incarcerate you if you overstay.

Bureaucracy, as the traveller sees it, maintains its territorial rights in every country. The tourist bureau promotes long stays and expects visitors to spend much money. The immigration bureau seems, by propagating paperwork and enforcing restrictions, to hamper tourism. Neither bureau interacts with the other, whether or not they are at cross purposes. Extending a visa, once in the country, means queuing and waiting for papers to pass from desk to desk with frustrating slowness. Arrival immigration officials seldom have authority to extend the standard period allowed.

☞ Personal Experience
The stories of inconvenience are legion. While we were in Hong Kong, awaiting a flight to India, the regulations changed. India suddenly required a pre-issued visa. The Indian consulate in Hong Kong refused to issue a visa in less than ten days even though we held confirmed travel arrangements due to begin shortly. Irritated, we went to Bangkok instead; there we found we could get the visa in an hour and therefore went on to India with no problem. It seems the visa officer in Hong Kong didn't like Americans. We never received the courtesy of a reply when we complained by letter to the proper authorities. We have not returned to India.

Nations allowing you to visit with nothing more than a valid passport require a simple entry form/card to be completed on arrival. All international airlines provide these forms before landing, and explain the routine customs regulations.

☞ Anecdote
Visiting Kenya thirty years ago, a colleague saw that he had to declare his race. He wrote 'Human' on the form. Soon after the aircraft landed a severe-looking official announced that an unfortunate mistake had been found in the arrival documents. Fresh ones were issued, for all to complete. Feeling relieved that the rest of the class did not know whose rash act had kept them all in, my friend wondered what word would be acceptable. He need not have worried. The new form did not ask the question!

CUSTOMS AND EXCISE

There are limits to the alcohol and tobacco each adult may take into a country: usually one litre of spirits and one of wine plus 200 cigarettes. (Between countries of the European Union the allowance is much more fluid.) Australia is very strict about importing anything resembling food, plants or endangered-alligator belts into the country. There are bins on arrival to dispose of the half-eaten cheese sandwich or apple you were saving in case you got hungry. My wallet or belt has never been examined to see if the original crocodile gave its permission.

Be careful about making fun of any country's regulations. They have their serious purpose. We do however sometimes disregard a bold sign requiring one to declare any currency over US$5,000. If I have US5,500, I will not declare it because I don't like to show (or even admit to) a bundle of cash in an airport. It is the money-launderers they are looking for, carrying big bundles, and the regulation does not apply to tourists carrying sensible amounts to be used for internal travel. See Chapter Eleven for information on cash, traveller's cheques and credit cards. (The latter two make 'technical infringements' unlikely.)

Certain countries impose a limit on the amount of cash you may bring in – or take out; the latter figure will sometimes depend on the amount declared on the way in.

HOMECOMING DECLARATIONS

To return with foreign purchases, or to ship some of them home instead, is a question that relates to your country's customs regulations. A phone call to the proper authorities *before you leave* will answer all your points directly. We prefer to get the information from source; never from someone who has been there, or a non-travelling travel agent.

If you are one of those who are only guilty if caught, I have no advice for you. Carriers or sellers of drugs take risks wholly beyond reason. Even stealing a smoke on an aircraft where it is prohibited is a risk defying comprehension – worse, surely, than driving after drinking too much. I report any infraction when I see someone endangering my comfort or life, without compunction. Singapore and Malaysia hang importers of a small quantity of hard drugs or of a medium amount of cannabis; with jail and the cane for minor amounts. Thailand has the death penalty but is less forthright in using it on foreigners.

Your own country is specific about the limits on imported goods – on your overseas purchases brought home. Most have a maximum, with duty charged on any excess. There are prohibitions on, for example, ivory goods when the country has signed the international ban on ivory in defence of the elephant. Plants, animals, foodstuffs and endangered animal products may be banned or closely regulated.

The average tourist is not involved in these matters. Purchases are usually articles of clothing and souvenirs. Items shipped back while you are away are classified as unaccompanied luggage. If sent by mail (see *Shipping It Home* in Chapter Eighteen), contents declared are taxed or not at the whim of the customs. Shipping by commercial carrier is more formal, and in some instances requires payment before the goods can be despatched from the port – or a broker to handle the import. Follow the rules; life is too short to waste time and possible incarceration sneaking around the law of the land.

IN SUMMARY
The paperwork and regulations are inhibiting for first-time travellers. But once you have a passport and the necessary visa, it is plain sailing – and becomes easier every time you travel in the future. Inform yourself, and follow the well-published rules and regulations as a courtesy to the country you are visiting. While you are a welcome visitor helping to improve your hosts' balance of trade, remember that you are also a guest.

Chapter Eighteen

SHOPPING AND COLLECTING

A temple in Sri Lanka where one of the Buddha relics is treasured is a scene you will want to remember. You will take a picture, keep a brochure, buy a postcard and maybe acquire a souvenir model of the site. Adventure memories and memorabilia are inseparable from travel; and then there is the sport of serious shopping. Shopping is what many would call fun and games. The products and markets of the world have tempted travellers since time immemorial. Marco Polo writes of the treasures in China and of the many gifts he took home.

Traders plied the Silk Road for centuries, trekking for months across passes to bring goods to the Middle East and returned home, their camels laden with merchandise. Ship captains sailed the Mediterranean in ancient days seeking to exchange goods between its ports. They were the early wholesalers, establishing bridge-heads and foreign enclaves to consolidate the trade.

Today the traveller has the fun of accumulating 'treasures' of clothing, art, literature and handicraft at source. Like the old traders, you can bargain with vendors for a single item, or for dozens of clever shirts to resell to your friends on return. Fortunately you need not own a camel or a ship today. Huge aircraft take you from one port to the other in hours. Local post offices will send everything home cheaply for you.

Some overseas tours are created for shopping sprees only: Los Angeles to Hong Kong; New York to London; indeed Harrod's in London runs an annual sale for overseas shoppers, subsidising the fare from various airports.

Package tours always have an afternoon free for shopping; the bus takes you to tourism-designated stores. There is a feeling that the tour director or bus driver is getting a commission. In fact a great fuss was made by a group of Singapore merchants recently. Certain Japanese tour guides were directing their clients into specific stores that had paid commissions to them. When their charges wanted to shop elsewhere, they were fobbed off with "no time" or "those stores not approved". These evils of the travel industry will not affect the Independent Traveller. As ever, do your own research and act accordingly.

UP-MARKET AND TOWN-CENTRE SHOPS

Up-market has the connotation of expensive. I prefer to categorise the finer shops, boutiques and department stores as those selling brand-name products at world-level prices. A promotional ploy draws attention to a fabulous designer-garment at an astronomical price. However that same shop will also display the latest styles in clothing at normal prices. There is often a sale-rack with something very special on it, a one-of-a-kind that will be a joy for many years in your wardrobe.

Major department stores are marvellous places to start your shopping in an unfamiliar environment. Classically they are old-line companies with fine reputations for quality and access to finer goods and services. We often book into a city hotel in the central business district (CBD in driver's lexicon) for the convenience of shopping. If one's travelling companion is bored by shopping, one may prowl the CBD alone while he or she enjoys hotel facilities such as health club and massage.

One big problem of shopping in foreign places is allotting time for proper investigation. The serious shopper should set particular days aside for this purpose. Leaving it to unscheduled free time will always lead to frustration. In a large city, a single day hardly allows you to get started, let alone see the major centres. Don't waste the time, be pragmatic. Create a schedule for the up-market places and leave part of a day, or a separate day, for down-market sport.

DOWN-MARKET BAZAARS

A woman will sometimes collect memorabilia by bargaining for a pair of bright coloured loose pants and a mismatched shirt, as in the night market of Chiang Mai. When she wears them to the next neighbourhood get-together on returning home, the ac-claim will be heartwarming. Name drop: "I just happened to be at the night market in Chiang Mai and picked up a few things." A green-with-envy look from a friend is ego satisfying.

Her man has always desired an Akubra hat from Australia, after seeing Greg Norman wear one at PGA golf tournaments. Showing the Arizona Cowboys what the Aussie wears when rounding up the cattle is the pride, joy and ego-boost of the international voyager.

The Independent (non-scheduled) Traveller has the time, and therefore the best chance, to ferret out the offbeat markets and bazaars. Some are traditional weekend-only gatherings of the merchants and rural vendors of clothing, food, local handicraft and flea-market type goods. The Chiang Mai market is a nightly affair in a multi-story car park, and there are many like it in Asia. The surrounding streets are filled with the carts of food and trinket hawkers. Inside are four floors of individual stalls, selling everything from high-fashion clothing to crocodile-tooth jewellery. Every Asian city, town and village has a large or small market of this sort with a spread of fascinating goods and services. You can have your fortune told, buy snake-oil medicine, get a 10-minute massage or take a sack of exotic tropical fruit back to the hotel to gorge on. If nothing else, the experience of walking through, smelling the cooking odours and watching and talking with the local people is well worth the time and effort.

The Victoria Sunday Market in Auckland is in a large covered building teeming with people. Stalls are laden with wonderful New Zealand food or piled high with sheepskin and wool products. It has counterparts in Melbourne and Brisbane. Tiny Broome, in Western Australia, has its bazaar on the church lawn every Saturday. Down Under they vary from massive collections of hundreds of vendors to local pockets of a score of open stalls with handicrafts and canned jams and jellies.

In the United States, the version now sweeping the country is called 'swap meets'. Europe has had similar open-air affairs for hundreds of years, once accompanying the battles of knights on the field of honour. In the UK, there are 'car boot sales' where roles are sometimes reversed. Professional vendors stock up selectively from what may or may not be household junk. Rural auctions are another matter, and a treat wherever you come across one.

Eileen loves the game of chase-the-bargains. Interesting clothing is often found in odd lots from international designers fabricating goods locally. Styles are up-to-the-minute, colours and fabrics are exciting. Prices are low, but the challenge is to recognise the better items, and make sure they are first-class merchandise though with prices far below the up-market boutiques. Negotiating prices is fair game for both buyer and seller; if they were too reasonable to start with, the game would be tame and uninteresting.

Part of the joy of foreign travel is getting out amongst the local people, and immersing oneself in their way of life. Language is never an obstacle to a buyer or vendor at any level. While up-market shops and goods are largely intended for high-spending tourists and well-to-do residents, the markets and bazaars with their remnants, and the smells (and sometimes stench) of the city, make for adventure. We have fond memories of eating fresh mangoes at a hawker stand in Kuala Lumpur's Chinatown *pasar malam*. Laughing with young people from an assortment of countries, dripping with the sweet juice, joking with the two women slicing stacks of the golden fruit – what more could the traveller ask?

Eileen has an interesting habit of discussing all of these probable good times with the taxi driver, coming in from the airport. He may want to sell you a morning tour of the city or a day's side trip to the remnants of a ancient temple. What my good wife wants to know is where is the best shopping and when is the big bazaar? There is a problem once in a while over what she means by the market, but diligence and perseverance win through. After all, there are still the porter, the receptionist and various waitresses to advise where the good stuff is.

☞ **Shopping Tip**
Bring cash to the local markets, for they seldom take credit cards. But don't expect to spend too much as the prices are not painful. Also, beware of pickpockets.

TRICKS OF THE TRADE

Make friends with the waitress at the breakfast table and ask about the best local shops. Men seldom know where to shop and the concierge will usually send you off to places like Double Bay in Sydney – an exclusive shopping area referred to by the natives as Double Pay. Sometimes you can identify local women in the lobby or restaurant wearing a cute something or other. A complimentary "what a lovely blouse, where did you get it?" will result in a quick friendship and local shopping advice.

TRUE COLLECTORS

Art enthusiasts, antique collectors and other special-interest people learn the paths to the galleries and museums in any country, usually armed with advice on people to contact.

My own enthusiasm is for bookshops, a wonderland where I escape from the best-seller lists of multi-million-copy authors. Tales of local history and antique books on pet subjects are treasures to be acquired.

SERIOUS SHOPPING

You will gain greatly from research before you leave home – into exquisitely woven silk carpets from Tianjin or old Wedgwood china in England, for example. Your local stores will provide comparison shopping to make sure you know something of the thread-weave numbers of the carpet. Your library will furnish you with the history of Josiah Wedgwood and his art.

FUN SHOPPING

This is for the rest of us common folk who merely like to buy some characteristic clothes, souvenirs for the family, tee shirts from every resort in the world, or interesting varieties of tea. Stop on impulse at a roadside stand, take in the bazaars and open markets, find out where the locals like best to shop – and look for the bargains. It may take nerve to stop when something catches your eye, disregarding the snide remarks of a companion or tour group. In major cities, don't hesitate to sheer off from the group, have your fun, and take a taxi back to the hotel when you choose.

FINE JEWELLERY

Jewels are a whole world in themselves. My background as a jeweller and Certified Gemologist entitles me to write at some length on this serious subject. Every country has its own source of unusual raw material, and/or talent, for creating jewellery. All have, also, their fine professional purveyors of heirloom jewels, as well as a horde of rip-off vendors concerned only with making a buck.

Beware of the 'Bargain'

Gold, diamonds and rare gems have their stable worldwide value levels. Nightly news broadcasts around the world quote the price of pure gold, within a few cents the same price in every market. Diamond production is tightly controlled at source by the De Beers cartel. Therefore differences in price will stem from manufacturing and marketing the products.

The impulsive purchase of a lovely strand of pearls or a magnificent ruby and diamond ring is a joy forever. Tiffany in America is probably the cheapest place to buy fine jewellery, allowing for variables of quality and value. If you desire such a treasure, seek out first the finest jeweller in the town. Then you can compare other sources. If your treasure costs thousands of dollars, do take the time to shop – and be very wary of the dealer who claims the price to be a third of the average retail value. If so, why is he selling it so cheap?

The words 'manufacturer', 'wholesaler' and 'retailer' are useless to you as level-of-price marketing descriptions. The vendor is a seller and you become a buyer for an agreed price. That price denotes the value of the jewel – what you, a knowing buyer, are willing to pay for it. You are acquiring the treasure because it is beautiful and you love it. The gem has meaning, perhaps as your birthstone or a gift of love, because of its everlasting durability. Never, never buy it because it is a bargain. Never, never take a second choice because that seems a better buy. Horrors!

Fine jewellery has a special meaning and attraction for the possessor. A rare gem with some history – regardless of its price – has beauty and durability as attributes. A royal amethyst of modest value in an antique gold mounting that has been handed down through generations has been loved with more meaning than a new carat-size diamond of considerably more cash value.

SHIPPING IT HOME

Carried away? Bought more than will fit in the extra fold-away duffel bag? Not to worry. Take the lot to the local post office, buy a box plus tape, and pay the postage to ship it home. Some countries are strict. The Philippines may give you a hard time. China wants to look inside the box before you seal it. But in Malaysia the hotel's porter or Business Centre will scrounge up a carton, paper and string, and ship it out for you. We have sent dozens of cartons home from the many countries we have visited. We remember only one box being lost.

Most post offices' package service is limited to specific dimensions and a 10-kilo maximum per parcel. The cost has a fixed plus a weight element. Verify the local system, as they may charge on block weights such as under and over 5 kilos, with anything over 5 charged as 10. Thus if your package weighs 5.1 kilos you will pay the top charge, so you might as well include a few more things. To be safe take the unsealed box to the post office, check the weight and postage, and then seal and address it there.

Check for freight forwarders when you have bulky items to ship home. All bona fide overseas purveyors of carpeting, furniture and large items have the means to ship the goods for you and know the system of export shipping. In some receiving countries, like the United States, it is sensible to enlist the services of a local customs broker or agent to collect the shipment, prepare the customs paperwork, clear the goods and arrange delivery to you. There is a service fee plus whatever duty is payable. *You must have certified copies of your invoice, and declarations of the exact origin and contents of the package.*

☛ Caution

Know the incoming customs regulations of your country before you leave it. A phone call or visit to your local customs office will provide the current information. Purchases within the specified limits create no problem. It is when you get carried away, and spend hundreds or thousands of dollars, that the regulations come into play.

SUMMARY

Veteran travellers and adventurers usually acquire a shopping hobby. Inexpensive oddities can be a lot of fun; they set one prowling. One of my daughters collects mugs, another miniatures. For a while in China, Eileen favoured unique pocket knives used mainly for peeling fruit, porcelain spoons and decorative tea cans. I specialised in old-style tales of Chinese lore, printed in English; and colourful posters and calendar prints. Their book-marks and paper-cut artistry are forever tempting: excellent small gifts for friends at home.

In all parts of the inhabited world, there is a never-ending supply of locally produced craft art. Everywhere one finds the inexpensive works of street artists, especially while prowling the night markets after dinner.

We have bought rice paper in China, rough handmade brown pulp paper in Bhutan, and marvellously decorative folding envelopes in Japan. Your stamp-collector friends are ecstatic if you pick out some pretties and send them on the face of a local envelope, cancelled in Lhasa or Kathmandu. My son-in-law requests only a paper-money note from each country we visit. An album of money samples, coins and bills is as interesting to friends as the endless snapshots we've collected over the years.

In Southeast Asia, Hong Kong and Singapore provide notable examples of international imports, international shops and international shoppers. Selling spills out onto most pavements (many of which are covered, cloister-like) and shops and stores are generally open well into the evening. Shopoholics could spend a week in a hotel and adjacent shopping complexes, in either country. Multi-level mall stores are surrounded by five-star hotels. And that doesn't include the special events in the cities.

Whether you are a casual or a dedicated shopper, enjoy the markets of the world. Savour the delight of bargaining for a treasure, whether it be a rare jade carving, a copy of a Dior gown or the newest tight-leg pants and turtle-neck casual combination. With such a collection you will have a small museum, rather than a large album, to enjoy for the rest of your lives – and to pass on. Inherited jewels and works of art will be cherished by generations of your descendants. Go forth on your adventures, and shop to your heart's and your pocket's content.

Chapter Nineteen

TRAVEL TIPS
FOR COMFORT LOVERS

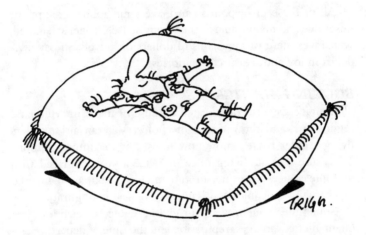

Besides our earlier advice on good health, travelling light and eating sensibly, there are many ways to enhance the physical comfort of long journeys. As we age, petty annoyances bother us more. Sitting for long flights in the narrow confines of an Economy Class seat stiffens the joints. The location of a room in the resort or hotel becomes important when you're staying for weeks instead of days. Special service in the coffee shop is appreciated if, for example, you like a big salad at dinner instead of a meagre bowl. However, creature comforts, expected and important in normal surroundings, are not always available if you're in the 'Tent Camp of Mountain Travel' in the Nepalese jungle.

You acquire information and make plans for months; or you just set out. You investigate hotels before you book locally, and

191

examine the menus that restaurants display; or you choose where to stay or eat, from booklets. Some travellers have a knack of being the Ugly American or Aggressive Taiwanese, with demanding arrogance; others cultivate friendly smiles with an appreciative 'Thank you.' A problem can escalate into heart-threatening aggravation, or be resolved calmly.

All of these pivot points can make your holidays happy, or miserable and memorable in the wrong sense. Properly handled, your investment of thousands of dollars on travel will pay dividends in joy and treasured memories.

BOOKING AIR TICKETS

The subject is very complicated because of the many rules and regulations, and the varieties of choice. Veteran air travellers flying regular routes know how to ask for maximum comfort. Adventure tourists flying once or twice a year are faced with multiple choices of airline, aircraft and price – but are hampered by changing schedules and ignorance of seat configurations.

Sometimes your travel plan gives a choice of airlines. Frequent-flier advantages, reputation and the time of departure and arrival vie for importance. We avoid late night departures because that day-in-waiting always seems to be time wasted. Hotels require midday check-outs, leaving luggage stored and preventing an afternoon siesta and last-minute shower. (But, for the first leg, it could be seen as a bonus day, at or near home, with all chores done and the morrow taken care of – an early start to the holiday, and then a night rather than a precious day given to the tedium of flying.)

Early morning departures are best, except when you have to fly in from a connecting point. Intercontinental flights always generate jet lag to aggravate a bad departure time or a West-bound flight. The correct way to compute time on a long flight, in your own mind, is bed-to-bed elapsed hours. In other words, the time you have to get up on the day of departure until the time you get into your next bed. In this context, waking up at a normal 7 a.m. and departing at midnight puts 18 hours on the clock before you start a long day's travel...

Sometimes you can't avoid it, but try anyway. Airlines often have different schedules according to the day of the week, because the beginnings of a route may vary. On a relaxed schedule you can choose whether to fly on Saturday or Thursday. Competing airlines alternate days with each other on certain routes to provide better commercial services. For instance Qantas flies Sydney – Fiji – Honolulu – Los Angeles. It leaves Sydney at a decent time, but if you pick up the flight in Fiji you depart at midnight. Air New Zealand, flying a similar route from Auckland, picks you up in the early afternoon. Thus you reach Los Angeles earlier without having to fidget for an additional eight hours before take-off.

One more travel tip. If you fly in from a connecting point for the major leg, leave the day before and sleep overnight at a hotel near the connecting airport. This shaves 12 hours off the bed-to-bed stretch.

Don't take the first flight schedule offered as final. If it's inconvenient, look for alternative days or airlines.

SEATING COMFORT

Efficient travel agents will sort all this out for you to the best of their ability. Unfortunately they're not all efficient, nor do many care whether you will spend nine hours cramped in the middle of a five-seat row. The aching-joint generation has a special problem, which most airlines recognise in their seat reservations.

There are two ways to handle this. One, if you are using an agent, is to be very specific. You would like a pair of seats for the two of you preferably in a two-seat row. Most big aircraft are configured two + four/five + two, across the cabin. By asking for windows, you'll seldom get stuck within a long centre row.

Additional leg room is often available in bulkhead- or exit-seats. Many airlines do not allow pre-check-in Economy Class seat reservations; however, if you can claim a physical condition such as arthritis, they will note that on your booking. The person checking you in should seat you accordingly.

One basic precaution helps immeasurably. Arrive at the airport at least two hours before flight time, to be first or early in the check-in queue. Smile nicely at the clerk, make a comment on why you always fly Malaysian because they are so nice, admire the lovely uniforms. Beg politely for a cosy two-seater exit or bulkhead row, with extra leg room next to a window, as far forward as possible. A friendly clerk will read your mind and will so place you that you will get out ahead of the crowd, reach the immigration check-in desk early and be first to the washrooms in the terminal. When you get good seats on an aircraft, note down the details and ask for them next time the same airline flies you in that type of aeroplane.

Eleven hours from Los Angeles to Tokyo nears a limit of 'tolerable endurance', even with the two meals, movies and lights-out sleep time. Even so, the 14-hour non-stop services between London and Singapore are more sought-after than the now old-fashioned, cheaper, stop-on-the-Persian-Gulf alternatives. In either case, break it up with freshening visits to the toilet (just before a film ends and the queues get long). Stretching exercises in the seat are good. Reach for the sky, clasp the hands behind the head and twist 10 or 20 times. When on your feet, go to the space near an exit and do some knee bends and *tai chi chuan* leg and arm stretching. (See Chapter Eight on in-flight exercise.)

Smokers and Non-smokers
Smokers will congregate in the rear of the plane, with or without specified seats. Domestic and short flights are all non-smoking now. Some airlines, weary of the struggle, have no-smoking seats even on long flights. But there remains a danger of the

addicted smoker, nervous in the air, sneaking a smoke, thus causing a scene and discomfort to nearby passengers.

It's the smokers now who have seating problems, because the airlines catering for both favour the large majority who don't smoke. They would rather have to displease a smoker than a non-smoker, when fully booked. *Avoid seats near the smoking section.* They are towards the rear, and provide the worst of both worlds; for while you *may* choke on the fumes from the seat behind, you may *not* use tobacco yourself. Discuss seat options thoroughly at the check-in desk, to make sure you have the best available seat for your comfort. *Reminder: arrive early to check in.*

DRINKING AND OTHER DIVERSIONS

Oxygenised air is very dry, therefore you need lots of liquid. Take everything they offer you and ask for refills of juices and plain water. The caffeine in tea and coffee will either calm you or keep you awake – whichever is usual for you.

Alcohol is the worst thing you can drink aloft on long trips because it dehydrates the body. A glass of wine with dinner is about all we ever drink unless on a short flight in a holiday atmosphere. Save a fascinating novel, bring a puzzle book if you're a word-nut; or cards or a chess board for games with your companion. If the newspapers issued are in your language, ask for a different good one each; for once, you will have the time to read them. Films shown may be to your taste, but we seldom watch them. The sound is often poor. With a 'big' screen, you crane your head either up, or round the heads in front.

The worst scenario is a child in the seat behind or in front of you, pounding away by the hour. It's no one's fault. Containing all that energy for more than half a day is more of a problem for a youngster than cramped seating is for older people. An under-standing comment to the parents will often help. If the plane isn't too full, the stewards may let you move to other seats, at least for a while.

SHORT FLIGHTS

When booking shorter flights on side trips, always ask for non-stop flights. Many domestic routes have intermediate stops that double travel time. For example, between Darwin and Broome, Ansett has one flight that stops twice and involves a change of planes; another schedule is non-stop. A helpful clerk will tell you of the choice, while another will put you on the first or least-booked flight on the list.

Higher class seats are more comfortable because of their size and special attention by the staff. However, with the Deluxe Economy travel that we suggest, a US$200–300 difference in cost can pay for two more days in a hotel room – a good exchange for the hour or two of luxury. It is on long journeys that higher class travel is worth considering, if you don't mind spending the extra money. We always conclude that those several hundred dollars would be better spent in extending our adventure, perhaps with another three days at a beach resort.

HOTEL ROOM LOCATIONS

We learned early in our travels to Europe that naive guests are usually offered the worst room in the hotel: next to a lift, over-looking an alley, or with a view blocked by another building. Sophisticated travellers always ask to see the room. For one night after a long journey, this is not important – if you can sleep. But on a second morning you want to wake up, throw open the window or step onto a balcony, and enjoy an enticing view. In a city a garden is prettier than a street, and quieter.

Hotel description verbiage is confusing. 'Standard' and 'Deluxe' mean the poorest accommodation, as a rule; 'Superior' is the average room; while the better and more expensive rooms are described as suites with or without further hype. 'Suite' is often a misnomer for an enlarged room with a pair of side chairs and a cocktail table. 'Double' means space for two people, except in China where the older hotels interpret it as two rooms.

You want the most comfortable room at the lowest price – or rather the best compromise between those aims, which we call 'Deluxe Economy'. Don't ask for that (or for 'Economy Deluxe', which relates to it as a half-empty does to a half-full bottle of wine), because hotel people won't know what you mean. Once you have stayed somewhere, write down the room number you want on the next visit, even if you didn't have it this time.

Our favourite hotel in Singapore is rated number one in Asia by certain professional graders. Years ago we used to have a room in the Garden Wing. It was mid-altitude, end of wing, large-balconied, away from the sometimes odorous cooking, and it looked out over the splendid lawns, pool and lagoon.

When the rates accelerated faster than our budget, we switched to the older Tower, with a corner room – a little larger, at half the rate, yet still overlooking the pool and garden. The legendary service prevails there no less, and the room maids even know us by name. They leave a liberal supply of 'decaf' coffee packets for the make-your-own facilities, and the fruit man manages an extra mango or two in the daily fruit basket. The Business Centre arranges my fax communications and always finds both an *Asian Wall Street Journal* and an *International Herald Tribune* for me. The freebies make up for the slightly enhanced cost of a fine hotel.

When reserving at a hotel new to us, we ask for a Superior room with a king-size bed, and a garden or beach view at middle height. On arrival we ask for an exclusive corner, or jokingly a honeymoon suite (for our 46th honeymoon). If they don't offer, we suggest a preview of available rooms. When we book in for a long stay, most hotels will upgrade the room at no extra cost as a courtesy. Chatting with the Reservations or the Duty Manager helps. Ask about the building's history; pay a compliment on the arrival procedures – in other words, make a friend. It works much better than arrogant demands.

Desirable room comforts include spaciousness, a refrigerator, international television, and coffee/tea makings. At resorts, a detached chalet away from the crowd and near the beach, with a porch and screened room for fresh air at night. We do not like to sleep in air-conditioning.

One last thought. 'Fully booked' is often used as a pretext for hotel clerks to place you where it suits them. It usually means they have a group-booking and the weekend is busy. Ask to see the Duty Manager and arrange to be switched to a better room after the crowd leaves on Sunday.

TRAVEL CLOTHES

Unless you are a film star expecting a posse of photographers, dress for comfort, not show. Loose-fitting clothes are the thing. By the time you have wriggled around an airliner seat for hours, tight-belted clothes and Fredericks of Hollywood underwear will have twisted the lower half of your body into excruciating knots. Feet swell, and Economy Class provides no way to prop them up. Wear casual slipper-style shoes that have room to go on and off easily. Sandals like our favourite Birkenstocks are admirable. If you're shy about walking into a posh hotel with 'barefoot sandals', carry a dressier pair at the top of your luggage and switch at the airport before you take a taxi.

Dress for the climate at your *destination*. You can leave Fiji in comfort with a light short-sleeved shirt, shorts and sandals, and find Los Angeles decidedly chilly that winter evening – especially if you walk a half-mile from the international wing to catch a domestic flight. We always travel with a lightly-lined nylon long jacket apiece, that can double as a raincoat or cover-up. They roll up in a small ball in our carry-on, or sit handily on top of the luggage when we arrive. From hot to cold, such as Singapore to Melbourne in the southern winter, you should have a jumper to hand, or wear warmer departure clothes. The airport is air-conditioned, and planes are often kept cold during flights.

SECURITY OF YOUR VALUABLES

Passports, boarding passes, tickets, baggage claim checks and entrance visas are bothersome. Everyone worries about wallets, credit cards and purses being stolen – and it does happen. For travel papers, the current vogue is waist pouches. They are unsightly but handy for the beach or on day tours. Leave the bulk of your valuables in the hotel safe or lock-box.

My system is to wear a shirt or jacket that has an easily accessible pocket to carry passports, entry forms and boarding passes. Everything else can be stored in a carry-on travel case. Women have their invaluable handbags. My side-pocket wallet holds enough currency to change at the airport, and one credit card. Everything else is locked in the carry-on case or money belt. Money belts are old-fashioned but the best possible way to carry extra currency and cards until you reach the hotel. For men, a side-pocket is better than one at the back because it is easy to keep a hand on the wallet in the pocket when walking through crowds.

On reaching the hotel, everything goes into the room safe or a safety deposit box at the reception counter. As for jewellery: wear it or stow it. Jewels in purses/handbags or left in drawers, earrings removed and set temporarily in the bathroom – these are at best cruel temptations to honest staff.

As mentioned in Chapter Eleven, there is now little need to carry large amounts of cash. A credit card gives you the best value for money so long as you don't run up interest charges. It is also an easy and reasonably economical way to draw money in foreign currencies. Traveller's cheques have superficial advantages; but do not buy too many, or cash them in hotels.

Be confident, choose your own travel systems, and follow them – but not so rigidly that they stop you from relaxing, and thus from enjoying the fun.

THE AUTHOR

Frederick and Eileen Fisher have the travel itch to see the faraway places with familiar names in comfort and a style known as Deluxe Economy. They constantly reorganize their lives to accommodate six months of travel pleasure each year. Retired now from the various careers of gemologist, jeweller and Chinese arts and crafts importer, Frederick now claims the career of author. Travel articles, a China travel guide, a novel, *Confucius Jade*, and new works constantly flowing from the laptop computer ensure a steady stream of the pleasure and interest in travel adventure.

Home for the Fishers is the crossroads ranch community of Sonoita, south of Tucson, Arizona, near the Mexican Border.

INDEX